Aylsham in the Seventeenth Century

Documents from the Manor of Aylsham Lancaster
researched by
Aylsham Local History Society

Pages 16 and 17 are folio 4 and verso 5 of document E.315/360, in the custody of the Public Record Office. The cover is a reproduction of the map which accompanies document E.315/360. We are grateful to the Public Record Office for permission to reproduce these items.

ISBN 0 946148 32 5

CONTENTS

ACKNOWLEDGEMENTS

Our thanks are due to the following:

To Christopher Barringer and Fiona Macdonald of the University of Cambridge Extra-Mural Board for their generous giving of time and expertise to this project; to Mary Manning of the Norfolk Research Committee and the staff of the Norfolk Record Office for advice at various stages of production, to Jane Key whose palaeographical and secretarial skills have been invaluable and, finally, to those members of the Local History Society and its committee for support and practical help in such necessary chores as typing and proof-reading.

FOREWORD

As a county Norfolk, despite the publications of the Norfolk Record Society, still has far too few major documents available in a form that can be used by those who are interested in its history but who are not able to deal with problems of palaeography and of translation from the Latin. It is therefore invaluable to have this Rental of Aylsham for the year 1624 (or thereabouts) produced in this accessible form.

The Aylsham Local History Society is to be congratulated in having concentrated on this document and taken its translation and analysis so carefully through to publication.

The Aylsham branch of the Workers' Educational Association originally invited me to look at the 'History of Aylsham' with them. We took the late Dr John Sapwell's excellent little History of Aylsham as our starting point. The Aylsham Collection assembled by Dr Sapwell and looked after by Mr Ron Peabody was our first archive. Ron, as curator of the Collection, retired Librarian of the Aylsham County Library Branch and Treasurer of the WEA Branch, was a key figure in all this preliminary research. Out of the second year of work by the class came Aylsham: A Guided Walk in which the WEA Branch members researched the detail, and the Aylsham Association, the Parish Council and Broadland District Council all co-operated in the production of the booklet. Shortly thereafter and as a direct result of these classes the Aylsham Local History Society was formed.

A copy of the Aylsham Rental had by this time been secured from the Public Record Office and it was realised what a splendid source it was for further study. At the request of the Local History Society the University of Cambridge Board of Extra-Mural Studies provided a course for this purpose. Fiona Macdonald, as a part-time tutor for the University of Cambridge Board of Extra-Mural Studies, was available to tutor the group. She did this most ably and the detailed work on the Rental got under way.

It is pleasing to see something that is the result of the co-operative work of so many people. It will be of lasting value and interest not only to the residents of Aylsham but to all who want to know more about the detailed nature of a seventeenth-century Norfolk community. All of those involved in the production of this study are to be congratulated on its publication.

Christopher Barringer
Resident Tutor in Norfolk
University of Cambridge Board of Extra-Mural Studies

INTRODUCTION

The document known as 'The Aylsham Rental' (Public Record Office E315/360) is an extensive manorial rental - a record of landholding in a portion of Aylsham - believed to have been compiled in the early seventeenth century (internal evidence suggests a date not before 1624). A small group of members of the Aylsham Local History Society have studied this document, initially in a Cambridge Extra-Mural Board class and subsequently in informal meetings over several years. It was felt that a summary of the rental, in English and in tabulated form, together with various analyses of the information it contains, might be useful to other people who were interested in studying the history of Aylsham and its inhabitants. The rental is a very rich source and would undoubtedly repay still further study.

At the time the rental was compiled, according to Blomefield,[1] there were four manors in Aylsham. The largest and most important was Aylsham Lancaster, which had been part of the Duchy of Lancaster estates since the Middle Ages. When John of Gaunt's son, Henry, became King of England in 1399 the Duchy of Lancaster estates were united with the royal lands and subsequently administered by the Crown. They were not, however, absorbed into the Crown estates, nor did they lose their identity. Henry IV instituted the 'Duchy Court' to control the administration of the Duchy lands, offices and perquisites. To this day, these holdings are distinct from Crown lands, and the Chancellorship of the Duchy of Lancaster remains a principal Office of State.

In 1401 the Duchy Court for the lands in Norfolk, Suffolk and Cambridgeshire was established in Aylsham, and Aylsham Lancaster became the capital manor of the Duchy for those counties.

This rental comes from the collections of the Exchequer Augmentation Office, which was concerned with the administration of lands acquired by the Crown. It is bound together with a copy of the lease of the manor for a term of 21 years from 1 July 1610. The recipients of this grant were William Neave and Thomas Leoman, gents. In the same volume is another rental, relating to one of the manors of Wymondham, Norfolk.

No reason is given in the rental itself as to why it was compiled, and it is not dated. However, it contains no references to land transfers after 1624, which suggests that it was compiled at about that time. Sir Henry Hobart purchased the Blickling estate in 1616. In 1622 the King granted Sir Henry a twenty-three year lease of the manor of Aylsham Lancaster, to commence at the expiration (in 1630) of the lease granted to William Neave and Thomas Leoman. Sir Henry was eager to purchase the freehold of the manor, and it seems likely that the Aylsham Rental was drawn up for Sir Henry by Edmund Reve, an Aylsham attorney and Steward of the Manor, in order to clarify the value and nature of the rents and profits of the manor prior to petitioning the King for permission to purchase the freehold. Sir Henry's son, Sir John Hobart, succeeded in this purchase in 1631.[2]

The other three manors mentioned by Blomefield were Vicarage, Sextons and Bolwick. The rental mentions the site of two 'former' manors in Aylsham (Bolwick and Calys) absorbed into the Duchy manor, although Blomefield makes no mention of a manor called Calys. It is not clear precisely how much of the parish was contained in the manor of Aylsham Lancaster, but it seems reasonable to assume that the tenants and their lands named in the rental constituted a substantial proportion of Aylsham's population and acreage, although its coverage was certainly not complete. As well as the tenants of the other manors, there would also be freeholders and landless people not named in the document.

The rental is written in Latin, in a clear hand, in keeping with a dating of c. 1625-30. Sample pages are reproduced in facsimile on pp.16-17. Entries in the original document are arranged in a systematic fashion, with each page divided into ruled vertical columns under the following headings: tenants by copy (i.e. of court roll); land; rent; value. The manuscript also includes several folios containing transcripts of other documents relating to Aylsham and two maps.

Each entry starts with the name of a tenant. Altogether 109 tenants are listed, of which 20 are women. A few tenants hold land jointly with one or two other people. A card index of the tenants has been compiled, which draws together all entries relating to each individual. This card index may be consulted by application to

Aylsham's Honorary Archivist. Most tenants' holdings were composed of several separate units of land and/or buildings. The dates at which each tenant entered into each unit of his or her holding are given. It is clear that, for many tenants, these units had been accumulated over many years, rather than having been taken up as one 'fixed' unit on a single occasion such as the death of a parent. It would be interesting to look for evidence of the reasons why tenants took up new holdings in the court rolls for this period. We know that the inheritance custom of the manor was gavelkind, by which property was divided equally among sons (or daughters). This might enable comparisons to be made with Margaret Spufford's work on the effects of differing inheritance customs in Cambridgeshire villages.[3]

Even if we cannot be sure of the reasons for land acquisition from the rental alone, it does enable us to discover something of the dynamics of land transfer. At an overall level, some years saw a substantially larger number of land transfers than others. At an individual level, it might be possible to divide many tenants' holdings into a 'core' containing dwelling house (messuage) plus outbuildings, arable land, and 'extra' units of arable, pasture or heath. There may be room here for further analysis.

Frequently the names of fields, streets and messuages are given, together with the dimensions of houses, barns and market stalls. There are references to neighbouring properties, roads and public buildings. Unfortunately, this topographical information is often not sufficiently comprehensive to allow any certain reconstruction of property boundaries, but it has been collected together for ease of reference on pp. 101-106. Those familiar with rentals and surveys of the medieval and early modern period will not be surprised to learn that many of the place names given in the rental 'disappeared' by the time of the earliest surviving large-scale maps of Aylsham in the early nineteenth century. However, further work on manorial records, wills and deeds from the seventeenth and eighteenth centuries may yet bridge the gap and permit some of the messuages, tenements and enclosures named in the rental to be identified on the ground. It is perhaps worth noting here, as an example, one of the most tantalising place names mentioned: the Old Market and Old Market Street. This was the site of several substantial buildings, some of which adjoined plots of land several acres in size. There are also numerous

references to shops and stalls in the Market Place, presumably on the same site as the present market place, which is bounded by many seventeenth-century buildings. Since this is in the 'obvious' place for a market to develop, i.e. at a point where several routes meet, and just outside the churchyard, one wonders where the 'Old' market place might have been.

The variation in size and value of the tenants' holdings is large, ranging from a single market stall with no land to the establishment listed as being in the hands of Charles Cornwallis (Royal Collector in 1604), which sounds very much as if it is the former centre of the Duchy's own activities in Aylsham. The holding, valued at £101.00, comprised agricultural land, a house of ten 'spaces' (presumably equivalent to the more usual 'bays' and used throughout the rental to indicate the dimensions of buildings), with a barn of eight spaces, a gatehouse, other buildings of 17 spaces, stables seven spaces, a wood-house two spaces, three yards, an orchard, a garden and a hopyard. Between these two extremes is a wide variety of holdings; see p. 73 for a tabulation.

The range of rents recorded is similarly large. On the whole, there is a straightforward relationship between the size of holding, the rent charged and its valuation. Further detailed study could perhaps discover more about the relative values of different types of land, although in many instances buildings, arable and pasture are all valued together in one 'package', with no separate rent or value given for each component. Investigations into the manorial court rolls for this period might reveal if, and by how much, rents varied over the years covered by the rental. According to the terms of the lease of the manor, some held their lands by fixed rents, whereas other, 'free' rents could be varied, presumably at the will of the lord. But there is no evidence within the rental itself to indicate how each rent had been decided upon, or indeed, if it had been re-negotiated at the time that the tenant named in the rental had taken up the holding.

It is interesting to note that many of the substantial messuages (of several bays) are not supported by a large acreage of land. It must be stressed that this is, at best, only a partial record of land-holding - some people might hold all their lands in other manors (in

Aylsham) or in neighbouring townships or in Norwich, Yarmouth, etc. Another possibility is that some of the inhabitants of Aylsham may have derived their income from non-agricultural activities, either in trade (? in the market) or in manufacturing, most likely in weaving or some aspect of the cloth trade. Some market stalls were held by people with no other property at all, whereas others were part of larger conglomerations of property held by one individual. Further study is being undertaken on wills and inventories for this period, and it is hoped to move on to study the surviving parish records, in order to find out as much as possible about the individuals named in the rental and their non-agricultural and non-manorial activities.

Where land is mentioned in the rental, not much detail is given as to its nature or use. Most agricultural tenants (i.e. those who held more than two or three acres of land together with a building) held a mixture of arable and pasture land. Some (presumably poor quality) land is described as being 'either arable or pasture'. There are frequent references to heath, moor and furze, and occasional references to marsh. The two most striking features of the plots of land described in the rental are (1) their small size (many are less than two acres) and (2) the fact that many of them are enclosed. There are numerous references to closes, both of arable and of pasture land. In addition, there are several instances of tenants holding re-united fragments of a larger unit of land; in other entries, there is evidence of a larger unit having been sub-divided and the separate portions enclosed. This is perhaps an indication of some process of rationalisation of holdings since some tenants seem to be gradually acquiring several separate plots in one particular area, as if they were trying to build up a consolidated block of land.

From the evidence of the rental alone, it is hard to discover anything of the field pattern in Aylsham, although field names are given (see p. 101). Enclosures were also being made on the commons, or waste land. This may have contributed to the need for the maps bound up with the rental. One shows lands along part of the Cawston/Aylsham parish boundary, with several closes of land identified as belonging to named individuals, and apportioned in 'diverse parcells of several heath' to 'diverse men'. Unfortunately, the plots of land shown on the map cannot be positively identified with any individual holdings in the rental, although some of the same tenants are named in both. The other map relates to the Blickling/Aylsham boundary, where common ground seems to have been disputed between 'Aylsham men' and 'Blickling men'.

There is a tendency for the size of landholdings transferred by copy of court roll and recorded in the rental to decrease over the time covered by the document. From the evidence in the rental alone, it is hard to say whether this is due to a change in the pattern of enclosure, related to a decrease in tenant prosperity, caused by the operation of gavelkind inheritance, or even by attempts to get round its provisions. As Margaret Spufford found, the attempt to keep the family farm intact and provide a cash share for younger sons could lead to financial crisis, and the eventual disappearance of the 'small farmer'.[4] The decreasing size of landholdings is an aspect that merits further study.

The rental, although limited in scope and partial in its coverage, sheds light on a wide range of topics of interest to the historian of early modern Aylsham. It is an excellent source of names of a considerable proportion of the population; and of many buildings, roads, fields and other topographical features. There is considerable information about the amount and value of the land that these inhabitants held from the manor, and about the types of buildings they lived in. The document displays the great variation in wealth among the tenants, although it must be stressed that they may have had other non-manorial sources of income or have held property in other manors. Aylsham market place is revealed as a thriving area with at least 27 stalls and a few built-up shops. There was a saffron ground, a market stead, a fairstead and a woolcross, and the town had washing grounds, all surely significant features in its commercial development. The presence of a fish stall suggests the existence of local fish ponds or perhaps links with the coast. There was a schoolhouse, a former workhouse and an almshouse. One house is singled out as having a 'faire parlour'. There was a gristmill and a malt mill.

More work still needs to be done before the rental has revealed everything it can about Aylsham in c. 1625. But because so much fascinating detail has already come to light, it seems appropriate to present a report on researches to date, in the hope that they may be useful to everyone interested in Aylsham and its history.

Fiona Macdonald
Part-time Tutor
University of Cambridge Board of Extra-Mural Studies

Notes

1. Francis Blomefield and C. Parkin, An Essay towards a Topographical History of the County of Norfolk, 11 vols. (London, 1805-10).

2. For the background to the negotiations between the tenants of Aylsham, the King and the Hobart family, see E. M. Griffiths, 'The Management of Two East Norfolk Estates in the Seventeenth Century: Blickling and Felbrigg 1596-1717' (unpublished Ph.D thesis, University of East Anglia, 1987).

3. Margaret Spufford, Contrasting Communities: English Villagers in the Sixteenth and Seventeenth Centuries (Cambridge, 1974).

4. Spufford, Contrasting Communities.

ABBREVIATIONS

ac.	acre
appurts.	appurtenances
bet.	between
cont.	containing
E.	east
ft.	foot, feet
mess.	messuage
N.	north
occup.	occupied
spac.	space, i.e. bay
sen.	senior
sep.	separate
S.	south
sit.	situated
W.	west
w.	with
yd.	yard

THE RENTAL (PRO E/315/360)

Description

As outlined in the Introduction, the intention has been to organise the data recorded in the Rental into a form from which meaningful information could be drawn. This has been achieved by arranging the details for each entry under various headings, each item of property being recorded on a separate line. Once this was done it was relatively easy to select specific categories of information, such as a list of land values, topographical features, etc.

Accompanying the Rental there are other papers: there is a copy of the lease of the manor to the tenants of Aylsham in 1610 by the King, and a copy of the Charter granted by King Henry IV allowing a weekly market and a fair on the feast of St Gregory the Pope. There are also some comments by the Bailiff who compiled the Rental on his findings concerning the customs of the manor and some of his observations about the church, the mill and the other manors in Aylsham. Bound in with the Rental is also a list of all the tenants of the manor, most but not all of whom are copyholders.

The maps on the outside cover are reproduced from the Rental, and represent two areas on the boundary in which the ownership was unknown or in dispute. One of these is Abel Heath, part of which was claimed by both Aylsham and Blickling. Today the Aylsham parish boundary still crosses the heath diagonally. The other adjoins the parish boundary with Cawston and is entitled 'The Brewerie Heath and Waste Ground of the Towne of Aylsham, commonly called Meadow Hurne or the King's Common Ground' (see contemporary documents, 'Dispute with the Queen 1600', pages 132-135).

The following two pages are a reproduction of the original entries in the Rental for Edmund Watts, which are summarised on page 25. His will and inventory have been transcribed, and appear on pages 125-130.

Tenentes per Copiam	Terr.	Redd:	Val.
Idem tenet per Copiam dat primo die Augusti in festo Sci Petri anno regni Jacobi Regis xij° Unu Stallag' iacen in foro de Aylsham contin in longitud xiij ped et latitud quinque ped et abutt super Stall Thome Spettue [illegible] et Aldermanni de Norw[illegible] Habend ut supra Redd per annum		j^d	iij s iiij d
Idem tenet per Copiam dat in festo Sci Thome Apple ~~[illegible]~~ xiij° Jacobi Re Unam peciam terr' cum stallag' de sup edificat nuper Rob[er]ti Websters contin longitud decem ped latitud quinque ped Habend ut supra Redd per annum		j^d	iij s iiij d
Idem tenet per Copiam dat die Sabbati in festo Sci Thome Apple xiiij° Jacobi Regis Unu Tentum cum Orto ~~[illegible]~~ eidem Spectan cum liber ingressu et egressu ad Hauriend aquam in Hungate streete con Habend ut supra Redd per annum	ptic iiij	ob.	iij s iiij d
Johes Hamde tenet per copiam Dat in festo Sci Marci Evang anno decimo quinto Jacobi Regis Unam Clausur terr' pastur cont p esti Habend sibi et assign sub Redd p ann	acr ss.	ij s ij d	xl s
Edus Watts tenet per Copiam dat die Sabbati in festo Sci Thome Apple Anno xiiij° Jacobi Regis Unam parcell terr' iacen in Starmans Crofte Contin Habend ut supra Redd per annum	acr iij	vij d	xxxiiij s
Idem tenet per Copiam dat die Lune in ~~[illegible]~~ Sci Marci anno Jacobi Regis			

Alysham / Tenent per Copiam. Terr Redd Val.

5

unu mesuag vocat the Swan cu
alijs edificijs w Swan hor 4 Swan ab
hor. in Swan cu orto adiacen-
stit in foro de Alysham et le
backsyde
Tenend sibi et Susanna uxor
eius Redd per Annum

iij ro p — j d. — xiiij s iiij d

Idem tenet per Copia dat
in ffesto Sci Thome Appli Anno
Jacobi Regis xo/
Totum ptem et pparte de et in
duodecem acr terr vocat
Tenend sibi et assign sub Redd
p Annum

j acr — vij d / — xliiij s

Idem tenet per Copia dat die
Lovis stilt in festo Sci Margaret
Anno Jacobi Regis xjo/
una pcell terr pcell unius
furlang vor Parsons close vocat
Tenend sibi et assign sub Redd p annum

j acr — viij d / — xxij s

Idem tenet p Copiam dat in
festo Sci Margaret Anno Jacobi
Regis xvjo/
unam pcell terr pcell firmacr
et dimid cu ffossat eidem adiacen vocat
duas alias pcell terr vocat p est
Tenend sibi et assign sub Redd p annum

j acr — iij acr p — iij d v d / — xls

Tho: Coates tenet p Copiam
dat die Lune stilt in ffesto Sci
Tho Appli Anno Jacobi Regis xvjo
Tres pcell terr iac in Stowgate
vocat p est
Ac tres per terr in quodam
Crofte vor Heath crofte vocat

iij acr p — v acr /

5 — 12 — 4

SUMMARY OF LANDHOLDING

AYLSHAM RENTAL PRO E315/360

Name	Date holding taken up	Description	Area	Rent	Value	Extra information including location
[page 1]						
Edward Mayes	1 August 1605	Parcel pasture	$2\frac{1}{2}$ ac	$9\frac{1}{2}$d	20sh	formerly occup. by John Diball
Edward Rye	1 May 1580	Stall in Aylsham Market Stall in Aylsham Market	12ft))) 8ft x) 4ft)	2d	2s 2d	next to stall formerly occup. by Flight next stall formerly held by John James
John Watson	1 August 1609	Cottage 'built up' with garden	10 perches	1d	4sh	part of a tenement, now divided
Agnes Aldridge formerly wife John Metton	21 December 1585	Stall now built up		2d	2s 6d	formerly Butchers stall next Wm Smith's stall to S. and Market Cross, on surrender Andrew Thetford
[page 1 v.]						
Katherina Scarboro	21 December 1608	Built up tenement in Netherhall St. and adjacent yard also $\frac{1}{2}$ a well upon land of said John [sic]		3d	6s 8d	now a sep. tenement but formerly one, marked by a boundary stone between highway called Netherhall St. on east

Name	Date holding taken up	Description	Area	Rent	Value	Extra information including location
Henry Woodrow	1 August 1618	Mess. called Haggas House with appurts., enclosed by walls on E. and S. sides plus: tenement with garden & orchard	12 perch	2d	10s 6d	formerly Thos. Clarke's
Henry Woodrow	30 March 1604	Mess. lying in Oldenwall in Aylsham	1 rood	2d	20sh	
		To the north, a furlong called Fussils Close & parcel of land 11ft x 1ft	11ft			in the way leading towards Blicklyng
Robert Bateman	1 August 1609	A close in Aylsham	12 ac	4sh	£4 14s 4d	between the land formerly Ralph Archer's and the land of Simon Smith to the east
[page 2]						
Robert Bateman	21 December 1608	Parcell arable or pasture land	$2\frac{1}{2}$ ac	12d	18s 6d	between land of Simon Smith on E. and John Some on W.
Robert Bateman	30 September 1607	A mess. 3 spac., barn 4 spac.	3 roods	21d	44s 6d	in Stonegate streete
		A parcel heath	3 roods			in Stonegate heathe
		Parcel of land	3 ac			on surrender of Robert Archer

William Tompson	1 August 1610	Part mess. with garden called Hubberte and others	1 rood	2d	10sh	wife Hellena pays each year
James Bell **[page 2 v.]**	30 September 1619	A parcel of enclosed land called Wallecroft A meadow	15 ac)))) 2 ac)	5s 4d	£6 8s 4d	between the way leading from Aylsham towards Barrow on the south joining Robert Alleyns land to the E. holds with Elizabeth his wife
Thomas Munday (clericus)	21 December 1593	A tenement now divided into 4 cont. 10 spac., barn 3 spac. called Hobbes with appurts., orchard and close adjoining An enclosed pasture called Bunnes	2 ac)))))) 3 ac)	2s 5d	40sh	situated in Hungatestrete
		A stall in Aylsham market A close on the heath called le Furr Close	)) 20 ac))		£8	
Thomas Munday (clericus)	24 May 1614	All parts and proportions, viz 8 parts of a mess.	½ rood	12½d	5sh	in Hungate

Name	Date holding taken up	Description	Area	Rent	Value	Extra information including location
[page 3]						
Robert Allyn	1 August 1604	A mess built up 3 spac. x 2 spac., stable 2 spac. with adjacent close and garden	3 ac)			lying on Easton greene
		Another parcel of enclosed land called Le Gravill Close	4 ac)	6s 11d	£8 6s 8d	holds with Elizabeth his wife
		Another close of land	9 ac)			
		Another mess. called Redd Fenne	3 rood)			
Richard Thompson	1 August 1606	A parcel of land with a tenement built upon it	7 perch	½d	3s 4d	at the great bridge in Aylsham
John Bradye	24 March 1624	A parcel land	3½ roods)			at Hungates Ende
		A parcel land	3 roods)			between the land of Christopher Tucke on the far side next to the land formerly of William Dannett on the N.
[page 3 v.]		A parcel lying in one piece	2 ac)	4s 1½d	£8 8s 4d	
		Heathland cont. more or less 3 roods	3 roods)			on the S. side of the way leading from Aylsham towards Heydon
		Two pieces	3 ac)			in Eastonfield in Aylsham
		Two pieces	4 ac)			between other enclosures in Aylsham abutting on the high-way leading out of Aylsham

John Bradye	24 March 1624	A parcel of pasture land	½ rood	12d		
Robert Coye	29 September - 5 October 1595	A shop or stall in Aylsham market	2 perch	1d	2s 6d	
William Baker	29 September - 5 October 1616	A close of land called Little Chamberlyns	2 ac	12d	14 sh	
William Baker	1 August 1617	A close of meadow	3 ac	12d	30sh	abutting on to the highway leading from Rayes Bridge to Easton green
[page 4] William Baker	1 August 1619	A shop with a little room above, parcel of a mess. A cabina with a little room above, next to the shop A little conclavum and a little room with part of the atrium of the adjoining mess. and yard	8 perches	4d	13s 4d	formerly held by Robert Tucke next to Aylsham market
John Jones	3 October 1608	A shop 7ft wide x 10ft long	70ft	¾d	12sh	next to Le Marketstead in Aylsham bet. the shop of Margaret Chosell to the N. and shop of Robert Coye to the S.

Name	Date holding taken up	Description	Area	Rent	Value	Extra information including location
James Gogle	30 September 1619	A mess. cont. 4 spac. with inclosed garden with liberty of drawing water				in Hungate streete
		A $\frac{1}{3}$ part of built up mess. with adjoining garden	$1\frac{1}{2}$ rood	20d	20s	in Hungate streete
		A $\frac{1}{4}$ part of a mess. or cottage It appears to cont. 2 spac.				in Hungate streete, formerly held by Thomas Keymer (defunct) He holds with James Smith and heirs
[page 4 v.]						
James Gogle	1 August 1614	A stall in market of Aylsham 8ft long x 5ft wide	8 x 5ft	1d	2s 6d	abutting on stall of Thomas Pettus citizen and Alderman of Norwich
James Gogle	21 December 1615	A piece of land with stall built on it 10ft long x 5ft wide	10 x 5ft	1d	2s 6d	formerly held by Robert Webster
James Gogle	21 December 1616	A tenement with garden adjoining it with free entrance and exit to draw water in Hungate street	4 perches	$\frac{1}{2}$d	2s 6d	

John Hannde	29 September 1617	A close of pasture land	5 ac	2s 2d	40sh	
Edmund Watts	21 December 1616	A parcel of land	3 ac	12d	24sh	in Starmancroft
[page 5]						
Edmund Watts	29 September 1617	A mess. cont. 6 spac. with other buildings 10 spac., barn 3 spac. with 'ort' adjoining and le Backsyde. Barn 4 spac.	$3\frac{1}{2}$ roods	1d	13s 4d	sit. in Aylsham market Holds with Susanna his wife
Edmund Watts	21 December 1617	All parts and proportions of and in 12 ac. land	6 ac	6d	44sh	
Edmund Watts	29 September 1613	A parcel of land, parcel of an enclosure called Parsons Close	2 ac	8d	16sh	
Edmund Watts	29 September 1618	A parcel of land, parcel of $3\frac{1}{2}$ ac. with a ditch adjoining 2 other parcels of land	2 ac) $3\frac{1}{2}$ ac)	4s 5d	40sh	
Thomas Coates	21 December 1618	3 parcels of land A second piece of land	$3\frac{1}{2}$ ac 5 ac			in Stonegate in a certain crcft called Heathcroft

Name	Date holding taken up	Description	Area	Rent	Value	Extra information including location
[page 5 v.]						
Thomas Coates	21 December 1618	2 parts divided in five parts (3 ac. + 3 ac. + 3 roods in 3 pieces)	6 ac 3 roods			in Stonegate
		An enclosure	1½ ac			
		A part divided into five parts in 3 pieces	3 ac 3 roods			in Stonegate
		A part and five parts lying in 2 pieces	9 ac	9s 11d	£21 8d 4d	in Stonegate
		A close called Sucklinge with a ditch and an outside (extra) ditch	2 ac 1 rood			
		The third part of 5 pieces of 3 ac and 3 roods	2 ac 1 rood			
		A mess. 2 spac. with a barn and stable 5 spac. now enclosed	16 ac			in Stonegate formerly Woode
		A parcel of land formerly heath	1½ ac			
		A toft 3 spac., a barn 3 spac., a 'stabal' 2 spac., with cottage 2 spac., with close and garden	2 ac 3 roods			in Stonegate

Thomas Hallifax	1 August 1615	A mess. built up 5 spac. with barn and stable 10 spac.and le backsyde	$\frac{1}{2}$ ac	5s 7d	20s	in the market place in Aylsham
		One piece of land called Leolland	2 roods			
		2 pieces in 3 divisions of a toft or mess. called le Tyled house and a garden				in the market place in Aylsham
[page 6]		Parcel of land	20 perches			on the S. of the said toft on the surrender of Thomas Some
		And also the third part of a tenement containing 2 spac.				formerly held by Edward March in the marketplace of Aylsham
		An 'officinam' called le Backhouse				formerly held by Thomas Clare deceased
Launcelott Thexton	1 August 1594	A mess. 3 spac. with other buildings 5 spac., a stable and 'le haie house" 2 spac. barn 3 spac. and 6 perches of land added to the said mess. with the yard	1 rood	23d	£3 8d 4d	formerly held by John Fletwell sit. of W. of market
		One piece of land with a stall 7ft long by 4ft wide in the market place	7 ac			
		One enclosure of land				next to John Orwell on the E. and the land of Robt. Skyssham on the E. and abutting on the highway to the N.

Name	Date holding taken up	Description	Area	Rent	Value	Extra information including location
Robert Tompson	29 September 1618	A tenement	10 perches	1½d	3s 4d	in Milgate Streete and abutting on highway towards the W., formerly Robert Botte's
Humphrey Holbye	29 September 1599	Arable or pasture land	1 ac 3 roods	12d	12sh	inclosed by the Vicar's land on all sides
[page 6 v.]						
Humphrey Holbye	1 August 1614	An enclosure of arable land and pasture	5 ac	2s 6d	30sh	
Humphrey Holbye	29 September 1588	One part of a mess. with a yard	½ rood	16d	5sh	in Hungatestreete
Humphrey Holbye	21 December 1609	A mess. (built up) 3 spac. and barn 3 spac. with le Backscoe and Backwaie with appurts.) A parcel of pasture adjacent to mess.)	10 ac)			in Stonegate streete formerly Humphreys
		An enclosed meadow belonging to same mess.	1 ac)	2s 6d	£5	lying bet. land of Simon Smyth on S. and land of Ralph Archer on N.

Humphrey Holbye	21 December 1609	One parcel of meadow belonging to the same mess. 2 pieces of land	1½ ac) 2 ac)			lying bet. land of Ralph Lawse to N. and S. lying at Stonegate and abutting on highway leading to Cawston on S.
Humphrey Holbye	10 April 1605	2 closes	7 ac	4½d	42sh	in West Field of Aylsham part of 14 ac.
Humphrey Holbye	1 August 1613	Half a stall lying in the market place	6ft	1d	2s 6d	
[page 7]						
Humphrey Holbye	3 October 1608	One pightle called Marsham gappe pightell	2 ac 3 roods	8d	13s 4d	
Humphrey Holbye	June 1588	Fourth part of a mess. in Stone-gatestreeete with all lands, meadows and pasture adjoining	10 ac	2s 9½d	3sh	in Stonegatestreete
Humphrey Holbye	10 April 1615	One piece of land in Eastonfield [deleted in original] Half a mess. with garden (gardino) and 'orto'	1 ac) 2 roods)	2d	18sh	in Eastonfield [deleted]

Name	Date holding taken up	Description	Area	Rent	Value	Extra information including location
Humphrey Holbye	1 August 1615	One piece of land in Eastonfield	1 ac	4d	6sh	in Eastonfield
		A shop in the market place	10ft	3d	2sh	
Humphrey Holbye	29 September 1587	A parcel of land and a ditch 'built up' and planted cont. 30 perch and 3 virgate long and one virgate wide, parcell of 7½ ac. and ½ a rood	2½ ac 2 roods)	) 17½d	20sh	in right of his wife
		Parcell of a mess.	20 perches)			in Market streete
[page 7 v.]						
Launcelot Thexton aforesaid		A pightle enclosed with a ditch with a barn now built	1½ roods	6d	6s 8d	he holds by will of his father
Launcelot Thexton	1 December 1595	An enclosure with 4 adjacent ditches	1 ac	6d	6s 8d	
Launcelot Thexton	1 August 1581	A piece of land lying in a close	2½ ac	9d	16sh	in West Field of Aylisworth (sic)
Gregory Breuiter	23 March 1620	A mess. 4 spac. barn 4 spac. stable 2 spac. another barn 2 spac. cum le Malthouse 2 spac. with gardens and 'ort' and adjoining close	14 ac)			

Gregory Breuiter	23 March 1620	One close and one dovecot called le Dovehous Close	2 ac	32s 11$\frac{3}{4}$d	£25	lying in Eastonfield
		Diverse other parcels of arable and meadow pasture	49 ac			
John Breuiter	– James	Diverse parcels of arable or pasture land enclosed	21 ac	paid with Gregory Breuiter	£6 6s 9d	lying in Aylsham
[page 8] Robert Rumpe	21 December 1554	A mess. built up 3 spac. barn 2 spac. stable 2 spac. called 'Dreeserrs' and a parcel of land, parcel of 14 ac. with orchard and garden adjoining	1$\frac{1}{2}$ ac	6s 11d	£8	land is lying in a certain place called Washinge yarde
		Divers parcels of enclosed land and other parcels of land with ditch	4 ac			on the surrender of Thomas Harrison; on the surrender of John Wood
		Other parcels of pasture land	6$\frac{1}{2}$ ac			abutting on Kaston Lane to the N.
		A parcel of land, parcel of 3 ac. in 2 pieces	1 ac			
Robert Baker and Martha his wife	26 March 1619	Divers parcels of pasture or arable land and meadow, parcel of 50 ac.	26 ac	11s 2$\frac{1}{4}$d	£8 8s	formerly Knighte
		A parcel of heath	1 ac			formerly Bewes
		Another parcel of heath	1 ac			formerly Tooks

Name	Date holding taken up	Description	Area	Rent	Value	Extra information including location
William Scottow		A tenement with apurts.	3 perches)			in Scottow
		A parcel of land	3 ac 3 roods)	9d	26d 8d	
		A parcel of land	$\frac{1}{2}$ ac)			lying in Scottow
Laurence Barr **[page 8 v.]**	27 March 1612	All parts and purprestures of and in 1 ac. called Cargrounde	2 roods	2d	4sh	
		Another half ac. lying there	2 roods	2d	3s 4d	
Robert Doughty (gent.)	1 August 1612	A mess. built up cont. 4 spac. barn 5 spac. with diverse other buildings cont. 11 spac. and other buildings 6 spac. with one Le Chauntry 9 spac. with Le Woodhouse 2 spac. with orchard, garden and le backside	2 ac)			in Le Olde Markett
			)	19s $3\frac{1}{4}$d	£16 3d 4d	
		Arable or pasture land lying in divers pieces and in diverse parts aforesaid	40 ac 1 rood)			in Aylsham
		Another parcel of pasture land	$1\frac{1}{2}$ roods)			
		Another parcel of pasture land	4 ac)			lying in the field called Cockerellfield

Robert Doughty	1 August 1612	Another parcel of land called Fayles Toft or Fayles Crofte	7 ac))			he has for his life and after his death his heirs and assigns will hold it in perpetuity according to the custom of the manor
Robert Doughty	1 August 1617	A close of pasture called Pyes Close	7 ac	6d	42sh	by the will of Robert Clare, father; lying in the Old Markett
Thomas Knowles	1 August 1619	A close of heath	10 ac	20d	£2	lying between the land of John Berker on the N. and the land of Edward Watts on the - side and the common way on the S. side

[page 9]

Thomas Knowles	1 August 1616	A parcel of land	2 ac	8d	12sh	lying in a certain close called le Little Close bet. the land of the Rector of Aylsham on the N. and the highway leading from the street called Churchgate to the Old Markett on the S. and abutting on the land of the said Thomas Knowles in part and the land of William Thompson and others in part on the E. side
Christopher Sankey	1 August 1619	A cottage with a garden	3 perches	$1\frac{1}{4}$d	2s 6d	situated in Hungate street

Name	Date holding taken up	Description	Area	Rent	Value	Extra information including location
Christopher Sankey	21 December 1606	A house and shop 14ft long by 8ft wide	14ft x 8ft	6d	12sh	holds in the right of his wife
Christopher Sankey	26 March 1616	A stall in the market 8ft long by 6ft wide	8ft x 6ft)	2¼d	12sh	
		Another stall in the market	)			holds through his wife
[page 9 v.]						
Simon Smyth (bailiff or reeve)	21 December 1587	A mess. built up 4 spac. barn 4 spac. with divers other buildings with their all and singular appurts.	1 ac)	16s 2d	£22 10s	in Stonegate in Aylesham
		Divers parcels of arable land and pasture	70½ ac)			lying in Stonegate (holds secundum consuetudinem salvo iure)
Simon Smyth	21 December 1597	A parcel of land called Westyard	1 ac)	6d	13s 4d	in Stonegate
		A parcel of meadow	1 ac)			in Norgate formerly Umfries (holds as above)
Simon Smyth	1 August 1596	A decayed stall in the market of Aylsham 8ft long by 4ft wide	8ft x 4ft	1d	12d	holds as above

Simon Smyth	1 May 1593	Half of 2 ac. of land or heath	1 ac	½d	2sh	formerly John Weltons and Berill his wife
Simon Smyth	1 August 1608	A parcel of a mess. 4 spac. with a parcel of the yard	1 rood	12d	12sh	in the street called Hungatestreete lying bet. the mess. and boundary
[page 10] Simon Smyth	1 August 1614	A toft 'ad opus et usum' of the said Simon	2 ac	5d	12sh	in Stonegate, next to Chamberlyns
Simon Smyth	1 August 1613	A close called Cobbs close	14 ac	2s 4d	£4 7s	
Simon Smyth	29 September 1618	A close of land	3 ac	12d	18sh	lying in Stonegate next to the land of Henry Coates on the E. and the land of Simon Smyth on the W.
		A piece of meadow called Priests Meadowe	1½ ac	11d	7sh	
Simon Smyth	1 August 1607	A close of land	11 ac	2s 3½d	£3 6s 8d	lying in the place called Estonfielde in Aylsham
Robert and Richard Swanne	1 August 1619	A tenement with an orchard and half a well	1 rood	1d	10sh	sited in Milgate Streete

Name	Date holding taken up	Description	Area	Rent	Value	Extra information including location
[page 10 v.]						
James Smythe	1 August 1600	Diverse parcels of arable land pasture meadow and heath	124 ac)			lying in Aylsham
		A mess. 4 spac. stable 3 spac. with other buildings 5 bay with orchard and gardens (ad opus et usus)	1½ ac)	12s 6½d	£37 10s	in Le West Fielde
James Smythe	1 August 1618	A piece of land called Larwoode Yarde	2½ roods	2d	3s 4d	in Hungate Street
James Smythe	1 August 1607	Diverse parcels of arable land meadow and pasture and heath	11 ac	2s 3½d	£3	holds with Johanna his wife
James Smythe	1 August 1618	A stall, i.e. a fish stall, 5ft long by 3ft wide	15ft	1d	3s 6d	situated between the stall of Humphrey Holby on the S. and the stall of Margaret Chosell on the N.
Robert Gurney	30 September 1620	A mess. or cottage 4 bay with orchard and garden	1 rood	2d)	14s 4d	in Milgate Street
[page 11]	1 April 1600	A mess. with the adjoining yard and pightle	3 roods	9d)		in the right of his wife

Simon Leverington	29 September 1618	A mess. 3 spac and other buildings 2 spac. with appurts. with the backside	17 perches	6d	4sh	situated in Hungate Street formerly Gregory Medcalfe
Simon Leverington	30 September 1605	A mess. built up 10 spac. with the outhouse and a faire parlor 5 bay barn 4 spac. with a garden and hort annexed to it and a close with a barn built upon it	$3\frac{1}{2}$ roods	2s 6d	30sh	situated in Hungate Street lying in Hungate Street
Simon Leverington	27 March 1618	A piece of land 7ft long by 4ft wide	7ft x 4ft	1d	2s 6d	lying in the market place to the west of a certain shop formerly Robert Clare's
Simon Leverington	24 March 1608	Arable land or pasture	3 ac)			lying bet. the land formerly of John Barker on the N. and the land formerly Thomas Clampe on the S.
		Another piece of land	3 ac 1 rood)	4s 6d	43s	lying in the field of Aylsham
		Another piece of land	2 roods)			in the same field at the southern end
		Another piece of land 12ft wide by 2 perches long	12ft x 2 perches)			

[page 11 v.]

Simon Leverington	1 August 1615	A piece of land	$2\frac{1}{2}$ ac	8d	15sh	abutting on the highway to the E. and lying between the land formerly of John Bradye senior deceased to the S.

Name	Date holding taken up	Description	Area	Rent	Value	Extra information including location
Simon Leverington	20 January 1617	A close	6 ac)			lying in the West field next to the land formerly of Robert Berker
		A close called Furre ground	6 ac)	3s 6d	£4	lying next to Jarvisbridge wood
		A piece of heath	10 perches)			
Simon Leverington	1 August 1608	A parcel of land	6 ac	2s 6d	37s 8d	lying in Hungate and formerly Thomas Meadowes parcel of 12 ac.
John Younges	26 March 1613	An enclosure of land	3 ac)			lying next to Cobb close
		A cottage 2 spac. built up, with the backside	2 roods)			formerly Robert Graunte's
		Another parcel of pasture	2 ac)	2s 7d	50sh	in Meadowehurne
		A parcel of heath land	3 roods)			lying in Stonegate heath formerly Robert Marsham
		Another parcel of heath	2 ac)			in Stonegate heath
[page 12]						
Thomas Lawes	29 September 1614	A mess. 5 spac. with all orchards and gardens	2 ac)			
		4 stalls in the market of Aylsham	)			

Thomas Lawes	29 September 1614	A close of pasture called Palmersdale	6 ac)	)	)	
		Another close	3 ac)		)	lying next to Brandledicke
		Another close called Hungate close	2 ac)		) £9. 12s	at the end of Hungate Street
		A piece of land	5 ac)	19s 9d	)	lying in the West field
		Another piece of land	1 ac)		)	in le Markettfielde
	29 September 1613	Arable land, meadow and pasture enclosed called Tudmore close	15 ac)		£4 10s	
	29 September 1611	A barn with garden and a parcel 'Funde'	1 rood)		2s 6d	lying in Hungate Street and lying outside the eastern wall which divides the said barn, garden and parcel of 'Fundi'
[page 12 v.]						
Thomas Smyth	1 August 1575	A mess. 3 spac. with 2 cottages and barn 2 spac. with an adjoining garden	2 ac	1d	26s 8d	lying in Hungate Street
Thomas Smyth	23 September 1580	A parcel of a decayed mess. and 120 ac. of land, meadow and pasture	60 ac	13s 4d	£18	lying in Moregate formerly Agnes Knightley's
		A mess. 3 spac.	10 perches	8d	6s 8d	lying in le Churchyarde

Name	Date holding taken up	Description	Area	Rent	Value	Extra information including location
Edward Brampton	1 August 1584	Six parts divided into seven of a mess. with curtilage annexed to it	80 ac 1 rood, viz:			formerly Thomas Skipping by the name of 80 ac. of meadow and pasture with reed beds containing one rood across the bank of the river in Aylsham and flooded by its waters
		A piece of land 60ft long by 12ft wide and at the southern end 3ft	½ rood			
		Divers other parcels of land	8 ac			
		Divers other parcels of land lying in Aylsham	28 ac			lying in Aylsham formerly Robert Walte alias Walters
		Another parcel of land	3 rood 37 perches	39s 2½d	£42 6s 8d	lying in Whittenharm
		Another parcel of land in 2 pieces	2 ac 2 roods			in Eastonefield
		Another parcel of land in 2 pieces	1 ac 2 roods			
[page 13]		Arable land in two pieces	1 ac 1½ roods			formerly Math(ew) Martins
		Another parcel of land	2 ac 2 roods			formerly John Bone's
		Another parcel of Cooke's land	2 ac 2 roods			
		Another parcel of land in 3 pieces	1½ ac			lying in Smalden

Edward Brampton	1 August 1584	Another parcel in 3 pieces	2 ac	at Beaneland
		A mess. built up with divers parcels of land adjoining	18 ac	formerly John Edmunds (sen.)
		A pasture called in English Backhouse with two virgates of land		lying on the W. side of the said pasture
		A parcel of land containing an enclosure	8 ac	formerly Jurdans lying at Bargebridge formerly Robert Watte's
		A parcel of marsh called Reade Fenn	2 ac	
		Another parcel of land	2 ac	formerly Coles in Eastonfield
				He holds all and singular these premises of the aforesaid Edward Brampton, his heirs and assigns according to the custom of the manor
William Orwell and Christiana his wife	1 August 1615	A parcel of land with a ditch	3 roods	formerly William Knolls
		Another parcel of land	2 ac	formerly Elizabeth Baxter
		A tenement 4 spac. barn 3 spac. called Paradise with certain lands adjoining	2 ac 1 rood	
		A close called Coursts with appurts.	2 ac	

Name	Date holding taken up	Description	Area	Rent	Value	Extra information including location
William Orwell and Christina his wife	1 August 1615	Another parcel of land with a ditch, way and passage and a mess. with appurts.	4 ac			formerly Anthony Norgate
		An enclosure	7 ac			formerly of the said Anthony
		An enclosure called Smythes close	17 ac			
[page 13 v.]		Another piece of land formerly enclosed in the last mentioned close	3 ac			
		Another piece lying in the said close called Smythes	2 roods			formerly Freman Lawes'
		Another piece of land	1 rood			formerly in Russells'
		Another piece	2 ac			lying in Choslee Croft
		Two pieces	1 ac			lying in the next croft
		Another piece of land 17yds long by 10ft wide at the southern end 8ft	51yds	22s 7d	£12 13s 4d	
		A parcel of land 44 virgates long, at the W. end 14 virgates	½ rood			in Westfield
		A parcel of a mess. called Le Overde	1 rood			on the west of the market

William Orwell and Christina his wife	1 August 1615	3 tenements, parcel of the tenement called Wickette		in 'Cennter' of Aylsham
		And all that capital mess. with all horts and gardens adjoining, viz: the mess. is 6 spac. the barn 4 spac. with other buildings 11 spac. a malt house 7 spac. with other buildings and 3 bay 8 'hor' there with an orchard containing 1 rood and a hemp-land 26 perches and le backsyde	1 ac	sit. in W. of market formerly Bostons
William Orwell [page 14]	27 March 1612	One piece of enclosed land in croft	11 ac	formerly Margaret Kinge's (widow), now in the tenancy of John Barker
		And another enclosure called le Reeds	12 ac	
		Divers other pieces of land now in 2 enclosures and now enclosed	$10\frac{1}{2}$ ac	
		And a piece of heath	12 ac	
		And another parcel of land	14 ac	
		A mess. 3 spac. barn 4 spac. built up with a garden	1 ac	in the street called Woodgate street
		Arable land in Aylsham field	15 ac	in Aylsham
		Another parcel of land	1 ac	

Name	Date holding taken up	Description	Area	Rent	Value	Extra information including location
William Orwell	27 March 1612	Another mess. with a close	$1\frac{1}{2}$ ac			
		Another parcel of land in 3 pieces	1 ac 1 rood			formerly Marlboroughs
		An enclosure of pasture	16 ac			
		An enclosure of arable land	1 ac 3 roods			lying next to the close of Robert Tooke
		Another parcel of land	1 ac			on the S. of Robert Tooke's
		And all heathland and other similar 'ungoverned land' (inordat) lying between the aforesaid closes		26s $1\frac{1}{2}$d	£37 6s 4d	herbage tenant
		A certain piece of land cont. 2 ac. and the ditch of Thomas Ashill on the heath	2 ac			as far as the bridge of Cawston
		Another parcel of enclosed land	15 ac			lying in Aylsham
		A parcel of land	$1\frac{1}{2}$ roods			lying in 'le Highe Furres'
		A piece of heathland	3 roods			in Aylsham and it abutts on the park of Cawston on the W. formerly of John Archer
		And another parcel of heath	1 ac			once belonging to Thomas Pye

[page 14 v.]

William Orwell	1 August 1613	An enclosure of land part of 4 ac. and 1 rood	3 ac	18sh		formerly Robert Clare's, lying in a certain 'Cennter' called Egmore's Stye to the W. Holds for the lifetime of Christiana his wife and it will then go to John Barker, son of Christiana
John Jostehus and Peter Barker	1 August 1615	A piece of land with adjoining parcel	2 ac			formerly Drewrie Hosted
		An enclosure	9 ac			formerly Harrison's
		And a piece of land there	3 roods			formerly ?
		Another piece	2 ac			formerly Lawes
		Another piece of land	1 ac			lying in Hethe Longe formerly John Brady
		An enclosure containing a meadow called Sucklings and 2 pieces of land	3 ac 3 roods			formerly Mundayes formerly Bollards
		A parcel of meadow called Sturmans Meadow 5ft wide by (the same in length as the whole meadow) i.e., 15 perches	12 perches	16s 7½d	£20 6s 8d	
		A mess. called Feanterres, viz. an enclosure	12 ac			
		A mess. built up 3 spac. barn 2 spac. called Gotte with divers land	16½ ac			formerly Henry Barker

Name	Date holding taken up	Description	Area	Rent	Value	Extra information including location
John Jostehus and Peter Barker	1 August 1615	An enclosure of heath called Wickette close	3 ac)			
		A tenement 2 spac. with adjoining close	2 ac)			formerly Rayners
		Another tenement 2 spac. cum 'le shead' 2 spac. cum enclosure	$1\frac{1}{2}$ roods)			
		And a shop with adjoining mess. with two stalls cont. 2 spac. a barn of 3 spac. with le backside	1ac)			formerly Spilmans
		A mess. called Wickette lying next to cennter 25ft wide by 4ft long	25ft x 4ft)			
[page 15]						
John Rymes gent and Elizabeth his wife	29 September 1615	A tenement 4 spac. called Chamberlyns with a garden adjoining and a parcel of meadow	2 ac	5d	20sh	lying in Stonegate Streete
George Soute	30 September 1619	An enclosure of land called Millbornes Close	$6\frac{1}{2}$ ac	$14\frac{1}{2}$d	40sh	in Aylsham
George Soute	27 March 1612	A mess. 4 spac. stable 3 spac. with le Seller and the yard	1 rood	4d	22sh	lying in Aylsham

George Soute	20 December 1620	A piece of a parcel of land called Cubberde Lyinge	3 roods	1d	4d	
William Harper	3 September 1619	A tenement	10 perches	6d	6sh	in Hungate Street
Francis (sic) Eastowe	27 July 1612					formerly wife of Thomas Skyffing now the wife of Robert Eastowe
[page 15 v.]		A mess. 4 spac. barn 5 spac. another tenement 5 spac. with other buildings cont. 6 spac. with an orchard and garden	$1\frac{1}{2}$ ac)			held by the last will of the said Thomas Skiffinge
		A parcel of land part of 120 ac.	$33\frac{1}{2}$ ac)			formerly of Richard Collyns
		Land, heath	1 ac)			formerly Thomas Everett
		Another piece of land	1 ac)	19s 8d	£17 12s	formerly John Witch
		Another parcel of pasture land	3 ac)			lying in the field called Markett field
		$\frac{1}{2}$ x 2 enclosures	7 ac)			
		Another parcel of arable land or pasture called Small yarde	9 ac)			lying next to the land of John Some
William Fisher	21 December 1619	Half a tenement now in 3 divisions cont. 3 spac. with a shop and Le Yard	11 perches)		6 sh	sit. in Aylsham
		Another half of the same tenement	11 perches)			formerly of Richard Cryfforde

Name	Date holding taken up	Description	Area	Rent	Value	Extra information including location
Richard Wilson	24 March 1615	A parcel of land	1 ac ½ rood	2d	8sh	lying in Markett field formerly Thomas Meadowes
	-	A parcel of land	2 roods	½d	3sh	lying in Eastonfield
[page 16]						
Richard Wilson	20 September 1619	A parcel of land with a built upon tenement	3 roods)			
		Another tenement with 'Atreo' adjoining	1 ac)			in Milgate Street
		A parcel of land	1 ac 1 rood)	5¾d	33s 4d	lying next to the heath called Sir William's land
		Another parcel	1 ac 1 rood)			lying next to the land now as then John Groute on the W. and the land of Robert Reymes on the E.
Thomas Cressy	29 September 1619	A mess. in Aylsham called Le Angell cont. 10 bayes and 2 tenements adjoining the said mess. with a barn of 5 bayes, 2 stables 5 bayes and Le Yard and Close adjoining	2 ac 2 roods)			
		A piece of land called le Ollandes	11 ac)	4s 6¾d	£8 7s 8d	formerly Robert Clare's

Thomas Cressy	29 September 1619	A piece of land of Furr ground	2 ac			lying next to the Heath
		A mess. called Greys 4 spac. stable 2 spac. and a parcel of meadow cont. 3 ac. and another parcel of pasture cont. 5 ac. adjoining the mess.	8 ac			
		A mess. and divers lands adjoining the mess. with the hemp yard	1 ac 3 roods			in Milgate Streete formerly Smythe's and Grixes cont. 12 inhabitants
Thomas Cressy	1 December 1610	A parcel of land called Wilsts	3 ac 1 rood	6½d	20sh	on the surrender of Thomas Clare
[page 16 v.]						
Thomas Cressy	21 December 1609	A mess.	5 roods			next to the Fairsteade
		Another parcel of land called Paysons	5 roods	7¾d	27s 6d	
		A parcel called le Fairstead	1 rood			lying upon Hollande
John Breuiter	1 August 1614	A piece of land called Jelions Rood	10 ac			lying bet. land of John Allen on the S. and the land of Thomas Munday clericus on the N.
		Another piece of land called Throughfer Close	7 ac	7¼d	£7	
		Another piece of enclosed land called Broomscroft	3 ac			

Name	Date holding taken up	Description	Area	Rent	Value	Extra information including location
William Unipher	-	A stall in the market of Aylsham 7ft in circuit		1d	3s 4d	abutting on the road leading out of the market
Margaret Chosell	22 December 1607	A built up mess. with le Brewhouse and Backhowse and other buildings cont. 10 spac. called Hourdardes with a close and le yard adjacent	2 ac)			
		A piece of land adjoining the said mess. called le Dam	1 ac)			
[page 17]		A built up shop in le Markett de Aylsham 10ft long by 8ft wide [crossed out in MSS]	10ft x 8ft)			
		A butchers stall cont. 40ft	)			
		Arable and pasture land in divers pieces	12 ac 31 perches)			formerly Joanna Rightwaies and Joanna Burrowe
		Arable land in 2 pieces	5 ac)			
		Heathland (enclosed)	7 ac)			
		Heathland (enclosed)	3 ac)			
		A close next to the highway	7 ac)			next to the highway
		Arable land	½ ac)			formerly Balles

Margaret Chosell	22 December 1607	A butchers stall 12ft long by 7ft wide	84ft			
		A built up shop 12ft long by 12ft wide	144ft			in the market of Aylsham
		Arable land	3 ac 1 rood			in Westfield
		Arable land or pasture in 2 closes	20 ac			in Westfield of Aylsham
		Arable land enclosed	7 roods			
				21s $6\frac{1}{2}$d	£24 3s 4d	
		More arable land	3 roods			
		Arable land	$\frac{1}{2}$ rood			in Westfield
		Arable land enclosed	3 ac			in Eastonfield
		Another stall	24ft			in le Markett de Aylsham
		Arable land	1 ac			in aforesaid fields
		A parcel of enclosed land	2 ac			
		A built house 2 spac.	20 perches			formerly a shop with orchard and garden
		A piece of land	20ft			formerly a shop which was burnt
		An enclosure				next to Willsegge
		A mess. 4 spac. barn 3 spac.	1 rood			in Hungate
		Arable land	$2\frac{1}{2}$ ac			in Eastonfield

Name	Date holding taken up	Description	Area	Rent	Value	Extra information including location
Margaret Chosell	22 December 1607	A cottage with the pightle and a parcel of land	1 rood)			in Munckeley in Eastonfield
		Arable land or pasture lying in 2 pieces	1 ac)			
		A shop built up	12ft)			in le Markett de Aylsham
[page 17 v.]		An enclosure of land and pasture	6 ac)			
		Arable land in 3 closes	6 ac)			towards Easton
		A barn 3 spac. with a close of arable land or pasture	3 ac)			
		A piece of waste 8ft wide by 7ft long	)			formerly parcel of one 'Le Looke'
		A tenement called Waggstaffe with the backside	1 rood)			
Robert Geagon (Armiger), John Orwell and Robert Doughty and others	28 March 1607	A tenement 3 bay now called Le Schoolhowse with a parcel of land next to it and a close called Paradise on the S.	2 ac	22½d	33s 4d	

John Orwell Junior, John Barker Junior, Thomas Hallifax, Simon Cressy and others	27 March 1618	2 built up houses (domus) 'elemosinar' (alms)			6s 8d	standing in a place in Aylsham aforesaid leading from Aylsham to Marsham. They hold these to the use of the poor and their heirs according to the custom of the manor. Rent paid by the grant.
Richard Smith	5 January 1619	All that land called le Heath Close	35 ac	3s 4d	£7	held to the use of the said Richard

[page 18]

Richard Smith	21 December 1589	A close	5 ac	20d	30sh	lying next to Cookrowshutte in Aylsham
Richard Smith	29 September 1612	An enclosure	6 ac	22d	36sh	adjacent to the close called kinge greene close part of 17 ac. formerly of Robert Mersham
Richard Smith	29 September 1607	An enclosure commonly unoccupied	12 ac	2s 4d	£3 10s	in Cookrowdale with a certain piece of land adjoining called Johns Hill
Richard Smith	21 December 1594	Two closes once in one enclosure called le Furre close	30 ac	2s 10d	£8 6s 8d	he and his heirs hold

Name	Date holding taken up	Description	Area	Rent	Value	Extra information including location
John Orwell 'Eliensis'	-	A mill called 'le gryst myle' and 'le malt myle'		£8 6s 8d		now in the occupation of Gregory Neale of Beningham standing 'under' a toft with a stable next to it and he holds it [new and later hand] him and his heirs at the will of the lord according to the custom of the manor etc.
Thomas Clare	26 March 1619	A tenement built up with a shop and half a well in le yard				formerly John Harrys
		With a piece of a parcel of land stretching as far as Horres and the aforesaid [piece] as far as the aforesaid well contains four feet wide		2d	12sh	with its appurts in Ludgate [Hungate] Street
[page 18 v.]						
Edward/Edmund Reve 'seneschall'	30 September 1620	A mess. cont. 6 spac. a barn 4 spac. with an 'atrio' annexed to it	1 ac			in the street called Old Market
		A pightle called Stones Howse	1 ac		33s 4d	
		An enclosure	2 ac			lying between the enclosure of Thomas Doughty on the E. and the close of Christopher Horne on the S.

Edward/Edmund Reve	21 July 1620	A built up mess. called Halls with le brewhowse 4 spac. barn 4 spac. stabul 3 spac.	1 ac		situated in Aylsham bet. the close formerly Stephan Drewry on the E. and Robert Hall on the W.
		A tenement or cottage 2 spac. with 2 pightles adjoining it	1 ac		
		A cottage built up with a parcel of land containing in length on the N. and S. side 24 rods and 1ft and in width on the W. and E. 29 rods and 2ft			with the liberty to take water from the stream
		A toft and cottage	2 ac 2 roods		lying at le old markett 'de antique' decayed, formerly Elizabeth Brackley
		A mess. built up 3 spac. called Marshall	2 roods	£8 6d 8d	formerly Stephen Drewry's
		All other customary lands of the aforesaid manor lying in closes	3 ac		
[page 19]		A tumbledown mess. and toft and appurts	1 ac 2 roods		commonly in the occupation of Tilneys
		One mess. and toft	1 ac		formerly Abraham Cookes
		Another mess. with a ditch	1 rood		on the W. side of the mess. and toft of the said Abraham
		One piece of land enclosed	3 roods		formerly in the tenure of Thomas Pecke
		All the lands of the aforesaid manor			held by copy of court roll lying in the said close, formerly of Henry Somes

Name	Date holding taken up	Description	Area	Rent	Value	Extra information including location
John Barker	1 August 1598	A mess. with appurts. called Bans	2 ac)			lying in Churchgate street in Aylsham
		Another mess.	2 roods)	2s 1d	£6 14s 4d	formerly John Wolsey
		2 other enclosures of meadow land and pasture	13 ac)			lying in Woodgate
Johanna Daye	4 March 1615	One parcel of enclosed land called le Saffron ground with a tenement built upon it where live 4 tenants	2 roods	1d	13s 4d	formerly wife of Robert Warren
William Kymer	20 July 1618	A meadow	3 ac		26s 8d	lying in Moregate in Aylsham to the 'work and use' of William Kymer. Rent paid by father
[page 19 v.]						
William Kymer	30 September 1607	Part 'of and in' $2\frac{1}{2}$ ac.	2 roods		3sh	
William Kymer	1 August 1612	1/5 'of and in' a mess.	16 perches		4d	formerly Henry Kymer his father's
William Kymer	24 March 1614	A tenement 3 spac. with barn 3 spac. and stable 2 spac.	3 ac)			in the street called Estonstreet

William Kymer	24 March 1614	with 2 parcels of land (arable) adjoining A pightle Another parcel of land	 3 roods 3 ac 3 roods	22d	£6 13s 4d	[also in Estonstreet] lying bet. the land of John Groute and Robert Allen
William Kymer	1 August 1617	A parcel of land	$8\frac{1}{2}$ ac	6d	50sh	in Eastonfield next to the kings highway leading from Kittlebridge to Brampton
William Kymer	1 August 1616	A tenement or mess. (decayed)	1 ac	$4\frac{1}{2}$d	20sh	now in the occupation of 'Samlyns'
Elizabeth Kymer	28 March 1595	A parcel of arable land part of an enclosure	$2\frac{1}{2}$ ac	3d	15sh	
[page 20]						
Elizabeth Kymer	1 August 1606	One fifth and part of a fifth of her proportion of a built up mess. One fifth and part of a fifth of a tenement part of the aforesaid mess. One fifth and part of a fifth of a shop		2s $2\frac{1}{2}$d	18s 4d	on the E. side of the church at Aylsham formerly Robert Gubbard in the market place at Aylsham
Edward Whitmore	1616	A piece of land 10ft long and 10ft wide with a shop on it		1d	6s 8d	in the market place of Aylsham

Name	Date holding taken up	Description	Area	Rent	Value	Extra information including location
Alicia Homes	27 March 1608	A cottage with le yard 10ft total length	8 perches	2d	8s 8d	holds for her lifetime and then it passes to Thomas her son
Johanna Akers	-	The other half of the aforesaid tenement	4 perches	2d	6sh	
[page 20 v.] Robert Thompson	1 August 1602	A tenement with an adjoining orchard	½ ac	5d	13s 4d	
Robert Wood and Anna his wife	28 March 1595	A mess. called Manor de Balwick 6 bays barn 8 bays stable 3 bays with other buildings 10 bays another barn 5 bays with pasture adjoining	8½ ac)			
		Arable land, wood, pasture, marsh enclosures, heath	42 ac)			
		Arable land and other holdings	46 ac)			
		A piece of land formerly in seven pieces	6 ac)			lying in Baldwick field
		2 pieces of land	5 ac)			in Skipping Crofte formerly of Croft Norgate
		5 pieces of land	3½ ac)			in the field of Baldwick

Robert Wood and Anna his wife	28 March 1595	A piece of land	$1\frac{1}{2}$ ac)			in Eastonfield
		A piece of land	2 ac)			formerly John Bennynton
		A mess. called le Manor of Calys	$1\frac{1}{2}$ roods)	60s $2\frac{1}{2}$d	£80	viz. 1 in the occupation of Mathew Godboult 2 in the occupation of Thomas Grix 3 in occupation of Adam King 4 in occupation of widow Bloefield
		Divers pieces of arable land and meadow and pasture	82 ac)			
		Meadow there	20 ac)			
		A piece of land arable	2 ac)			in Pyecroft
		A parcel of meadow there	1 ac)			
[page 21]		A close of meadow	1 ac 1 rood)			in Aylsham
		Another piece of meadow	2 roods)			formerly Thomas Rampe
John Pye	29 September 1595	A cottage part of a mess.	2 roods		8s 6d	formerly Robert Keaton
Robert Harmor	29 September - [Elizabeth]	A stall 7ft long by 4ft wide	7ft x 4ft		4s 6d	in the market of Aylsham
William Harmor de Sheyfield	29 September 1595	A stall (butchers) built up	30ft square		4s	lying to the N. of another stall formerly William Smyths (next Cruceny) in the market of Aylsham

Name	Date holding taken up	Description	Area	Rent	Value	Extra information including location
Peter Empson	3 March 1620	All one quarter part of five divisions of a shop			3s 4d	in the market of Aylsham; to the use of the said Peter and his heirs
[page 21 v.]						
Thomas Leoman and Emma his wife	2 May 1610	A capital mess. with barn, stable, orchards, gardens and divers les outhouses	2 ac 2 roods)			in Stonegate
		Another mess. called Silks and Mansers 5 spac. barn 7 spac. stable 3 spac. a mill house and brew house 6 spac. an orchard and garden with a croft and a little pightle adjoining	$10\frac{1}{2}$ ac)			
		A parcel of land	$16\frac{1}{2}$ ac 1 rood)			lying in Ostbrand heath
		Another parcel of arable land	4 ac)			formerly Thomas Least
		Another parcel of land with a mess. built up 3 spac. and 2 cottages 4 spac. with le meadow plott	2 ac)			formerly Christopher Horne in Stonegate
		A parcel of land	$3\frac{1}{2}$ ac)			in a certain close called Ten Acres close in Linckfield
		Another enclosure	2 ac)			formerly Christopher Allens

Thomas Leoman and Emma his wife	2 May 1610	Another built-up mess. 2 spac. shop 3 spac. stable 3 bays with le yard and adjoining close	$2\frac{1}{2}$ ac	£25 18s 4d	formerly John Okes
		Another parcel of land	5 roods		in the West Field formerly Christopher Tucke
[page 22]		Another parcel of land	3 ac		formerly John Woodwards
		A parcel called Seaven acres Close with Le Sponge	7 ac		
		A parcel of land called Appleheath Close	4 ac		
		An enclosure called Candle Close	$1\frac{1}{2}$ ac		
		A parcel of land part of Cokowdale enclosed	1 rood		
		A cottage (built up) 2 spac	1 rood		formerly Ann Skeytons
		A parcel of land	5 roods		in Westgate field formerly Nicholas Barkers. To have and to hold to the aforesaid Emma and her heirs which came to her on the death of her mother Dorothy Oxburow widow of Thomas Oxburow her father
Thomas Leoman and Emma his wife	27 March 1618	A mess. 4 spac. with an orchard and garden and a parcel of pasture land called Rumps	2 ac	15sh	held by Thomas alone

Name	Date holding taken up	Description	Area	Rent	Value	Extra information including location
Thomas Leoman and Emma his wife	27 March 1618	A pightle of land	1½ ac		9sh	in Aylsham held by right of Thomas and Emma jointly
		A shop called Le Woolcrosse 9yds x 9yds	)			in the market
		A pightle called Hoberte pictell	1 ac)		20sh	
		2 parcels of heath	1½ ac)			
[page 22 v.]						
Alice Reymer	1 August 1612	A tenement	4 perches	1d	3s 4d	in Hungate Streete in Aylsham she holds for her lifetime according to the custom of the manor
Robert Ventere	21 December 1618	A tenement with le backside with a close 'across the road'	1½ ac)	20d	£4 13s 4d	
		Divers parcels of land arable and pasture	12 ac)			
Emma Smythe	-	A piece of land	7 roods	7½d	6sh	on Aylsham heath
Rachell Norgate	21 December 1588	A mess. called Boy cont. 6 spac. and 'le yard'	20 perches)	) 18d	7sh	in the market place of Aylsham, to go to her sons Robert and William

Rachell Norgate	1 August 1599	A garden with a cottage upon it 1 spac.	10 perches))		4sh	next to the Pinfold in Aylsham
Robert Gelle	1 August 1612	A mess. 4 spac. with 'le Smythes Shoppe', barn 2 spac. with an orchard and close adjoining	1 ac	1d	20d	to go to William Brook
Elizabeth Wadlowe	1 August 16[?]	A built up tenement with le backsyde	13 perches	4d	3s 4d	
William Moore	25 April 1609	A stall in the market	12ft	1d	2s 6d	
Robert Curtis	30 September 1620	Arable land	4 ac	$5\frac{3}{4}$d	16sh	in East field
Thomas Harwood **[page 23 v.]**	- 1612	A mess. with barn 5 spac. and a close	3 ac	7d	30sh	
		Arable land	3 roods)			in Northcroft
			)	$\frac{1}{2}$d	18sh	
	1 August 1612	Arable land in 'aforesaid field'	$2\frac{1}{2}$ ac)			in 'aforesaid field'
Nicholas Brayde	24 March 1614	Arable land containing a cottage with a close (enclosed)	4 ac) 1 ac)			in Hungate
			)	$6s\ 1\frac{1}{2}$d	16s 8d	
		Arable land	$\frac{1}{2}$ ac)			in Palmers dale
		Land and pasture in divers pieces	$4\frac{1}{2}$ ac)			in Hungate Street

Name	Date holding taken up	Description	Area	Rent	Value	Extra information including location
Gregory Whissiter	– 1618	A stall	12ft x 12ft	1d	2s 6d	
Gregory Whissiter	– 1614	A stall	6ft x 4ft	1d	2s 6d	
Gregory Whissiter	1 August 1615	A pightle	1 ac	2d	6sh	in Markettfield
Gregory Whissiter	– 1610	A pightle	½ ac	1d	3sh	
[page 24]						
Edward Allene	30 September 1605	A mess. 3 spac. and barn 4 spac. called Dowes with appurts.	2 ac)			
		Arable land in divers places	20 ac)	2s 3d	£8	
		A mess. with an enclosure	2 ac 10ft)			
		A pightle of arable land	1 ac 1 rood)			
Edward Allene	– 1612	An enclosure of arable	4 ac	16d	24sh	

Edward Allene	– 1614	A tenement with an orchard	1 ac	13d	14sh	
William Corker	16 March 1620	A tenement	15ft x 12ft	3d	6s 8d	almost (tantum) in the market of Aylsham
William Greene	– 1600-1601	A tenement with le backsyde	3 roods	2d	8sh	
Robert Bussell and Christiana his wife	1 August 1619	A close of Arable land called Wattecroft	16 ac		£4 6s 8d	
[page 24 v.]						
Robert Bussell and Christiana his wife	29 September 1619	A tenement called le Workehouse now 2 tenements with a certain parcel of land called le Little yard	6 perches)	1½d	10sh	
		A cottage with a certain parcel of land adjoining and free passage to a well there	1 rood)			formerly of William Linsey
Rowlande Turner	– 1609	A cottage 5 spac. with the backsyde	20 perches	1½d	5sh	
Christopher Creessye	30 October 1608	Heathland and 'Jampum'[?]	1½ ac	4d	6sh	

Name	Date holding taken up	Description	Area	Rent	Value	Extra information including location
Christopher Creessye	- 1596-1597	Arable or pasture land	2 ac	6d	8sh	
Christopher Creessye	28 March 1595	A tenement 3 spac. barn 3 spac. with the backsyde	1 rood	$7\frac{1}{2}$d	30sh	
		Land with a barn built upon it	2 ac			
		An orchard and a piece of land 30ft wide by $10\frac{1}{2}$ perches with buildings built upon it				

[page 25]

Name	Date holding taken up	Description	Area	Rent	Value	Extra information including location
Thomas Norgate (gent.)	21 December 1619	His share of approx. $2\frac{1}{2}$ ac. (more or less) lying in 4 pieces in Aylsham, part of 8 acres in divers pieces in the West Field	4 ac			by the last will of Anne his mother in the West Field
		A piece of land, parcel of 9 ac.	3 ac			lying in Sturman's Close
		Three pieces of land in the West Field	2 ac			in the West Field (by the will of his father, as follows)
		His 2 pieces and proportions of and in a close cont. $3\frac{1}{2}$ ac. parcel of the close called Sturman's	$3\frac{1}{2}$ ac 2 roods			in the close called Sturman's
		Also another parcel of land in 5 pieces in Aylsham	6 ac			in Aylsham

Thomas Norgate	21 December 1619	A mess. 4 spac. barn 3 spac. and stable 3 spac. called Hylls with the Homestalls adjoining	4 ac			in the street called Old Market
		Another piece of land in Sillcrofte	3 ac			
		Another parcel of land, parcell of a mess.	1 ac	10s 4d	£16	
		And divers pieces of land	$9\frac{1}{2}$ ac			in Aylsham
		A close called Hylls close	5 ac			
		A mess. built up with a parcell of land adjoining	1 ac			
		Another parcel of land cont. in length	26 vergat			
		A mess. built up 6 spac. with a garden and a rood of land	1 rood			in Old Markett
		Another piece of land (enclosed)	2 roods			
		$\frac{1}{2}$ x 5 ac. of land lying in 4 pieces	2 ac 2 rood			part of 8 ac. in the West Field
		All parts and proportions of Henry Norgate and Edward Norgate 'de and in' an enclosure called Sturmans	9 ac $\frac{1}{2}$ rood			Henry Norgate and Edward Norgate sons and coheirs of the Professor of Sacred Theology

Name	Date holding taken up	Description	Area	Rent	Value	Extra information including location
[page 25 v.]						
Margaret Chosell	1 August 1620	A mess. built up with barn, stable and parcel of enclosed land adjoining	3 ac)			
		Arable land	3 rood)	2s $5\frac{1}{2}$d	30sh	in Sturman's Close
		Arable or pasture	1 ac 1 rood)			next to Brundale Ditche
Margaret Chosell	1 August 1617	Divers parcels of land, meadow and pasture	$3\frac{1}{2}$ ac	3d	20sh	adjoining the tenement called Greys
Thomas Empson	– 1613	A mess. built up with the Backsyde and other buildings containing 13 bays	$\frac{1}{2}$ ac	18d	8sh	
John Pricke	1 August 1617	Quarter part of a mess. built up, quarter part of a piece of land called 'Le garden plott' in Aylsham, quarter of a tenement vacant, and also an 'edificia promissore' viz. a hall, kitchen, shop, stable and yard all containing)	$\frac{1}{2}$ rood	2s $\frac{3}{4}$d	6s 8d	in the market place in Aylsham; in the market place
[page 26]						
John Pricke	1 August 1619	A stable with a little house above	$\frac{1}{2}$ rood	4d	4sh	

Henry Some	21 December 1615	A built up mess. 4 spac. stable 4 spac. 3 barns 7 spac. with other buildings 5 spac. called Woodgate with all appurts. adjoining with divers pieces of land, meadow, pasture and heath	38 ac			in Aylsham formerly of John Eldred
		Another parcel of land in 2 pieces	9 ac			at Stonegate
		Another half part of 3 [?] ac. next to the mess.	1 ac	14sh	£17 17s	
		Another parcel of land	1 ac			at Stonegate
		Another half part of the three ac. aforesaid	1 ac			
		An enclosure lying bet. the highway on the S. and the land of divers men to the N.	4 ac			
		Another parcel of land lying bet. the land of divers men to the W.	1 ac 1 rood			
		Another piece of land	2 rood			bet. the land of John Some
John Some	– 1618	Arable land plus heath plus pasture	27 ac	6s 6d	£7 10s	

Name	Date holding taken up	Description	Area	Rent	Value	Extra information including location
[page 26 v.]						
William Kilby and Johanna his wife	28 March 1617	A mess. 3 spac. with orchard	3 roods	8d	10sh	
Richard Tompson	– 1603	2 tenements with an orchard adjoining	1ac 1 rood	2d	6sh	
		Pasture land	3 roods	2d	3sh	
John Cobb	1 August 1614	3 cottages with tenement called Hyndes 5 spac. with orchard and garden	2 ac	1d	20sh	
Robert Foster and Margaret	1 August 1576	Arable land in field called Cockerellfield	2 ac	6d	12sh	for the work and use of their sons called Robert and Thomas
		$\frac{1}{2}$ close called Parsons Close	2 ac	6d	12sh	
Alice Godfrey	29 September 15[?]	A tenement 4 spac. with appurts.	20ft	8d	11sh	
[page 27]						
Mildred and Martha Baker	29 March 1621	$\frac{1}{3}$ part of mess. and stall	6 perch))			in Market of Aylsham

Mildred and Martha Baker	29 March 1621	Divers parcels of arable land and pasture enclosed	62 ac) 2 roods)	11sh	£19 6s 8d	in the fields of Aylsham
John Durrant	1 August 1620	A shop or tenement 2 spac.	2 perch		4sh	in the Market Place in Aylsham, formerly of John Richardson
Thomas, Richard and James Smyth	2 August 1621	2 pieces of heath	5 roods)	$7\frac{1}{2}$d	10sh	next to 'le great farr close'
		Another parcel of heath	2 roods)			
John Some	2 August 1621	A parcel of land with a barn built upon it	1 rood		4sh	formerly Jells at Sills Moore
[page 27 v.]						
Thomas Puttocke	21 December 1614	A mess. called Great Edmonde with an adjoining garden	1 ac)			
		Another parcel of land	15 ac 1 rood 8 perch)			in Willsegge in Aylsham
		Another parcel of land	6 ac 1 rood)			bet. land called Tobies Rood to W. and abutting on le Howardsclose to the N.
		An enclosure	2 ac)			in Crofto Mess.
		Another parcel of land	3 roods)			at the end of Willsegg
		Another enclosure of pasture	3 ac 1 rood)			formerly Andrew Thetfords

Name	Date holding taken up	Description	Area	Rent	Value	Extra information including location
Thomas Puttocke	21 December 1614	Another parcel of land	2½ roods	)	£8 6s 8d	part of 16 ac. in Eastonfield
		Another parcel	1½ roods	)		formerly of Robert Clare
		A pightle of new enclosure	2 roods	)		
		3 other parcels of land	5½ ac	)		in Eastonfield formerly Christopher Knowles
		Another parcel of land	6 ac 1½ roods	)		at Hungate
		Another parcel of land	1½ roods	)		formerly of Robert Clare bet. lands of Thomas Munday clerk to the S.
Johanna Haund	29 September 1616	A tenement	½ rood			wife of Robert Bette at le Old Markett
[page 28] Margaret Furmery and John Furmery	28 March 1611	⅓ tenement 5 spac. with garden	10 perch	14½d	3s 4d	
Anna Thurston	– 1618	A mess. 2 spac. a shop, a barn 2 spac. and le workehouse and garden adjoining	½ rood	1½d	6sh	

Robert Rayner	21 December 1590	A mess. 4 spac. a shop 1 spac. 18ft long by 1ft wide) Another piece a parcel of Le Loke which Loke is 18ft long and 6ft wide)		$16\frac{1}{2}$d	5s 6d	in le Markett of Aylsham
Nicholas Bradye	- 1613	A piece of land de Furrgrounde	3 roods	1d	4sh	lying in the place called Appleheath
Jacob Rayner	- 1594	A cottage with le Backsyde 10 perch long and 2 perch wide		$4\frac{1}{2}$d	3sh	
Johanna Elles	29 September 1571	A cottage 3 bay with orchard adjoining	32 perch	$2\frac{1}{2}$d	5sh	formerly Demmes

[page 28 v.]

Sir Carolus Cornwallis	-	A capital mess. cont. 10 spac. a barn 8 spac. a gatehowse and other buildings 17 spac. with stables 7 spac. and le woodhouse 2 spac. and 3 yarde, orchard, garden and le hopyard	4 ac)		£101	'He saie all his evidences was in the Court of Wards'
		Divers parcels of meadow land in enclosures	20 ac)			
		Divers other separate parcels of arable land enclosed	112 ac)			
		With divers parcels of pasture land enclosed	100 ac)			in the several fields of Aylsham

Name	Date holding taken up	Description	Area	Rent	Value	Extra information including location
						[New handwriting starts here]
John Orwell	1 August 1586	A mess. with its appurts	1 rood			built up in Myllgatestreete
		All of that land and meadow cont. 60 ac. 3 rood 20 perch, of which 6 ac. 2 roods have been sold, therefore remaining are	54 ac 1 rood 20 perch	6s 2d	£20	formerly in occupation of Robert Brewitor
	1 August 1592	A parcel of land	1 ac		26s 8d	in a certain stadio next to Paynters Bush
		Other pieces of arable	2 ac			in the fields of Aylsham
[page 29]						
Edward and George Pettus	–	[page blank]				[marginal note as follows:] He hath severall lands held off sundry Lords wheirof the Prince lands by the rent of 25s 8d but the tenants would not sett it forth: for now holds at gratia [=free; by grace]
[pages 29 v, 30 and 30 v. blank]						
[page 31]						
Edmund Haunde	1 August 1593	A parcel of land in 3 pieces with a tenement 2 spac.	2 ac	6½d	10sh	in Skornestone

Edmund Haunde	1 August 1598	A parcel of land	2 ac	1½d	12sh	in Skornestone bet. the land of Edward Haunde on the N. part
Thomas Edwards	1 August 1606	A parcel of enclosed land (customary) called Pattinstile Close with a pightle to the W. end of it	2 roods)			bet. the Vicar of Scottow on the S.
			)	13d	26s 5d	
		A mess. 3 spac. with its appurts.	2 roods)			in Scottow
		Another parcel of customary land	½ ac)			
John Warnes	1 August 1602	A parcel of customary land part of 2 ac.	2 roods	½d	3sh	
[page 31 v.]						
Edmund Moulton	1 August 1611	A cottage	½ rood)			in Scottow
		3 pieces of enclosed land	3 ac)	3s 9d	50sh	in Scottow
		Another parcel of land	4 ac)			in Scottow on the surrender of Hellen Stubb to hold for himself and his wife Dorothy
Robert Spendlove	29 September 1577	A mess. with barn 7 spac. stable 2 spac. and all other premises with adjoining enclosures	2 ac	4s 6d	25sh	in Scottow

Name	Date holding taken up	Description	Area	Rent	Value	Extra information including location
Peter Welles	1 August 1611	A tenement 3 spac. and one piece of land	½ rood	1d	5sh	he holds to his use and of Dorothy his wife
[page 32]						
Christopher Teylles	1 August 1609	Arable land	2½ ac	5d	10sh	called Skeytonfield
William Woodrowe	1 August 1606	3 acres customary land	3 ac	10½d	18sh	in Skeyton
William Church	23 March 1620	A parcel of pasture land	3 roods	½d	2s 6d	
		A piece of land called 'le head de le Toft'	2 ac	4d	8s 6d	in Skeyton
[page 32 v.]						
Thomas Allyn	2 May 1610	A parcel of land	7 ac 1 rood	2s 4d	50sh	in Eastowfield in Marsham
Thomas Allyn	1 August 1611	A mess. built up 3 spac. with a yard to the S.	8 perch	9d	5sh	part of the Cennter de Aylesham
[page 33]						
Hevingham						
Agneta Walker	1 August 1616	A parcel of land	2 roods	2d	2sh	wife of William Snellinge in Heavingham

James Gedge	29 September 1609	A parcel of customary land, the residue of a mess. called Spendlove Another parcel of land	½ ac) 5 ac 1 rood)	2sh	45sh	in Heavingham
[page 33 v. blank]						
[page 34]						
Marsham						
Agnes Horne	7 January 1614	A mess. built up with orchard and garden adjoining	1 ac	2d		holds freely by charter to hold for her lifetime and then to revert to James Horne her heir and assign to hold in chief etc.
John Warnes	7 August 1601	2 parcels of arable lying there	2 ac	12d		holds by charter holds as above
Agnes Black	10 April 1602	A house called le Clarkhowse of Knotts tenement, with a parcel of land part of 1½ ac.	1 ac	2d		holds by charter holds as above
[page 34 v.]						
Scottow						
William Lubbock	26 August 1606	5 parcels of land lying in a close called 20 acres	2 ac 3 roods	7d		holds freely by charter holds as above

LEASE OF THE MANOR OF AYLSHAM

Page 35 William Neave and Thomas Leoman, gentlemen, hold by indenture under the great seal of [the Duchy of] Lancaster dated First day of July in 7th year of King James for the consideration of £60 of lawful money and an annual increment of rent of 40/- the perquisites and profits of court of the lordship specified hereinafter. All that their manor of Aylsham in Norfolk with its rights, member and all appurtenances, with assised rents, new rents, lands, escheats of certainty there, the leet at Brampton Hall and Skeyton with the profits of the same as are now answered for. Also the perquisites and profits of the Court falling within the said manor and all and singular messuages, houses, buildings, orchards, gardens, tofts, cottages, mills and rents, barns, stables, dovecotes, pond, wine-store, land, tenements, demesne lands, meadows, pasture, pasture ('pascua' and 'pastura'), common wastes, furze heath, moors, marshes, fisheries and a (?) fish-trap ('piscacio') and Court Baron, Court Leet, view of frank pledge and all things appurtenant to the view of frank pledge, and the perquisites and profits of the same, fines, amercements, heriots, reliefs, serfs male ('nativos') and female ('nativas') and villeins ('villanos') with their offspring, fairs, markets and all the tolls of the same, and the assized rents and free rents of each bond and customary tenant there, and other services, rents and profits belonging to the said manor; and all rights, jurisdictions, easements, profits, emoluments and hereditaments of every sort, with all things appurtaining or

Page 35v belonging to the said manor in any way (lately leased to a certain John Trench, esquire, feodary and bailiff of the aforesaid community), except all great trees, mines, quarries, rights of fowling, hunting, etc.

To have and to hold all that same manor with its rights, members and all appurtenances (except those things excepted) - to the aforesaid William Neave and Thomas Leoman and their Assigns from the Feast of the Annunciation of the Blessed Virgin Mary last past before this present date to the end of the term and for the term of twenty one years from then following and fully to be completed, paying rent for the said assise rents, new rents, lands, escheats of certainty, leet at Brampton Hall and Skeyton aforesaid with their profits } £37.5s.0¼d.

And from and for the said occasional perquisites and profits of court, four pounds of old rent and forty shillings of new increment, viz. in all £6. } £6.

And the aforesaid farmers for themselves their heirs, executors and assigns agreed that they shall adequately repair, sustain, scour, fence, ditch and make and maintain all the premises when need be. And that the said farmers, their executors and assigns shall have and take sufficient and adequate "howsboote, hegeboote, fyerboote, plougheboote and Cartboote" of, in and upon the premises from any parcel thence arising, extending from time to time during the said term at their own costs and expenses, and when it shall be necessary, for the necessary repairs and use of the premises and to be used there and not elsewhere during the said term.

Page 36

And if it happens that the foresaid annual rents of forty-three pounds five shillings and one farthing shall remain unpaid for the space of forty days next after each of the said feasts, that the lease and grant aforesaid shall cease and be of no effect.

Assignment of this indenture was made to Nathanael Bacon, Knight, John Heavingham, Knight, Thomas Oxborowe, Nicholas Horne and George Gawdy esquires and their executors and assigns for the term aforesaid.

CHARTER FOR MARKETS AND FAIRS - HENRY IV (1399-1413)

Page 37v Henry the fourth of England by the grace of God to our beloved and faithful Bailiff of our town or desmene of Aylsham part of our Duchy of Lancaster in the county of Norfolk and to the inhabitants of the said town or desmene. That their heirs and successors there annually in perpetuity shall have and hold and be able to have and hold within our town and desmene aforesaid, a market every week on Saturday and a fair similarly there every year for three days duration viz. on the eve, the day and the morrow of the feast of Saint Gregory the Pope.

Paying to us and our heirs faithfully conceived and answering for all outgoings, profits and tolls of the same market and fair from wherever they came without increase paying from the start of this grant. 6s 8d

GENERAL COMMENTS BY THE COMPILER OF THE RENTAL

Page 38 By view of divers antient Rentalls they saye that their are sundry Freeholders which oweth suite and payeth Rente unto his Highnes whose names and Rentes are before incerted in this booke . . .

The Tennantes of this Mannor did some 10 yeardes since take a lease of the whole Mannor with all the royalties and profittes of Courte Fayr merkett etc in the Name of Certayne Feoffees by them named for 21 yeards soe that after the expiration his Highnes will Receive all the profittes which will amount to a greate vallew as by the [?]Rates of their landes etc maye in the booke appeare: Within this Mannor their is due unto his Highnes a Heriott custom which as the Tennantes pretend are not otherwise due to the Lorde except he payeth aboue a halfepenny Rent viz For the landes lying in Aylysham after the death of Every Tennantes they are to paye for a Heiriott Two shillinges Eight pence for certentye and For landes lyinge in Scottow beeinge a member of Aylysham yf it be a whole Toft Tenn shillinges yf lesse Two shillinges Eight pence and for landes lyinge in any other out Townes helde by Coppye of this Mannor beeinge more or lesse Tenn shillinges and as for Custom workes due unto his Highnes I cannot Finde that ther is any but they affirme that their Fynes are certaine but by view of their Courte Roules I Finde many diffirences arysinge boeth in their Herriotts and likewise in their Fynes with many probabilities to the Contrary And that their is payde For a common Fyne or certentye of the Leete yearely Fower shillinges six pence wheirof the Tennantes of Brundell paye 2s the Tennants of Scottow 2s & the bayleife 6s

They affirme that by their Custom the Coppyhold landes doe discend to the Brothers alike and soe to the sisters and Auntes as Coheires accordinge to the nature of Gauilkinde and they saye that the wyfe ought to haue the one halfe of the landes for hur dower after the Discease of hur Husband although she marry againe but they doe not allow any Intaile neyther doeth any holde by [Cu]rtisie neyther cann I Finde that any haue ayliened their coppyholde into Freeholde

Page 38v Their is not any Mannor howse within this Mannor but their is [a] peece of grounde lyinge towardes Causton Heath called the Kinges [Common] cont 60 acrs now in Lease to Thomas Coates incerted in a Plott before [. . .] per Annum 30s: And One other peece of grounde called Apple heath [cont . . .] worth 10s: one peece of waste at Oldemerkate cont 3 acrs 6s One other [piece] of Grounde at Easton Greene cont 2 acrs worth 12d One other [piece] called Goslwell cont ½ acr worth 6d one other peece lyinge at Muc[. . .] 4 acr worth 6s one other peece of grounde at Stonebridge 4 acrs [. . .] one little peece of grounde called Kinges Greene neere Cookowdale which be his Highnes butt the Tennantes neere Inhabitinge haue [. . .] common of pasture in them tyme out of minde Respectiuely and [s . . .] as they pretende as belonginge to their severall Tennementes tyme out [of] minde And for any Parke chase Demeaselandes woodes or other [. . .] then aforesaid their is not any as I cann Finde

Their is not any Patronyage Free de guifte presentacon or Nomin[ation] within this Mannor but the Presentacion to the vicaredge of Aylys[ham] hath beene heeretofore Questioned betweene his Majestie and the Dean [and] Chaptor of Canterburie and Mr John Huntt is now Vicar their worth [. . .] Annum

I Finde that their are certaine Escheate landes within this Man[nor] which is paid yearely 2s 3d but wheare they lie by whome they Escheated or how they cam to be Escheated I cannot Finde

Their are Fower severall Courtes kepte yearely for his Highnes First on Lamas Daye and the second uppon the next daye after St [Michael] Tharkangell which bee Courte Leetes the third on St Thomas Daye and [the] Fourth aboute the Feast daye on the Anuntiacion of the Blessed [Virgin] Marye wich be Courte Barrons the proffittes of all which haue vsually amounted to Fower Poundes per Annum or theirabouts as they [pro . . .] the which the Farmors of the said Mannor Answereth to his [Highness] six poundes per Annum Their is One Mr Robt: Woodes Esq which hath the

[. . .] of Balwick Hall held of his Highnes Mannor of Aylysham and ly[eth] within the same by Coppy of Court Rowle and keepeth Court Barron with the same Mannor. The said Robt Wood is ouner of another [. . .] in Aylysham called Aylysham: Sextens and alsoe the Vicar of Aylys[ham] for the tyme beeinge in the Right of the Church is alsoe ouner of [. . .] nother Mannor in Aylysham called Aylysham: Vicaridge to all which [. . .] a greatest part of the landes and Tennementes within the said Mannor and they doe keepe severall Court leetes and court Barrons within their seuera[ll]

Page 39 I Finde that their is one watermyll as they pretend within the Mannor which is held by John Orwell of Ely gent in Feo farme payinge theirfore yearely £8 6s 8d to his Highnes, hee hath since built up anothir watermyll aboute one yeare since for his priuate Benifytt of grindinge of Molte and theirby it may be thought that in Continewate of tyme he will compel the Tennantes of the said Mannor to grynde their molt at the said Myll contrary to all former vse and Custome their is not any cther mylles within this Mannor but the other lordes haue water mylles within their Mannors.

Their is one Merkett weekyly kept on Satterdaye within th[is] Mannor and one Fayer yearely kept on the Feast Daye of St Gregory the Pope the Euen before and the Daye after which were graunted under the greate seale to the Bayleife of the said Mannor and to his successors for the tyme beeinge which is paid per Annum, 6s 8d to his Highnes.

I Finde the wafes strages and Fellons goodes is properly belonginge to his Highnes and that the Baylefe of the Mannor for the tyme beeinge taketh up the same and that John Orwell of Ely beeinge Bayleife tooke up two stray horses and sold them: but wheither he answered to the Lord for them I cannot Find One Robert Doughty gent since deceased tooke up one Straye Nagg and sold him for 20s whoes Executors keepeth the same not knowinge wheir to paye it wheither to his Highnes or to the Right Honourable Sir Henry Hobart Knight and Barronet as Bayleife to his Highnes for the Dutchey of Lancaster of the Leasses of the said Mannor of Aylysham but they are Ready to pay out wheir it is dew.

Their is one Cottage erected on the waste by the Inhabitants 20 yeares since lying at stone Bridge vallue 6s 8d per Annum and other them that their is not any.

Their is one small Riuor within this Mannor the profitt of the Fishinge belongeth to his Highnes and is not in Farme to any as I cann heere but is of some worth yf it were disposed of.

Page 39v They affirme that the Tennantes within the Towne of Ayly[sham] duringe all the tyme of their Remembrances haue paid unto [his] Maiejestie or his Farmors for the tyme: for the Fyne of a m[essuage] or Tennement - 4d - for the Fyne of every acre of lande [. . .] and for every stalle and the Forren tennantes haue overpa[id . . .] for a Fyne - 4d the acre

I Finde that this Mannor is within the Dyoses of [Norwich] and within the Hundred of South reppingham and the T[enants] and [?]Reciantes are not called to be of any Juries out of [. . .] said Towne but onely to the visitacions of the Archbis[hop] of Canterbury the Bishop of Norwich and the Archdeacon their

The Limmites Buttes and Boundes cannot be sett F[. . .] but by plott by Reason other lordes landes lye intermixed [. . .] his Highnes landes their and doeth extend into other out T[. . .] neere adioyninge:

AYLYSHAM ALPHABETT – MSS index of Names of Landholders

A	page no.
Aldridge Annis	1
Allin Robert	3
Akers John	20
Allins Edward	23
Allin Thomas	32

B	page no.
Bateman Robert	1
<u>Idem</u>	2
Bell James	2
Brady John	3
Baker William	3
<u>Idem</u> William	4
Breuitor Gregory	7
Breuitor John	7
Baker Robert	8
Burr Laurence	8
<u>Idem</u>	8
Brampton Edward	12
Baker John and Joseph	14
Breuitor John	16
Barker John senior	19
Brady Nicholas	23
Baker Mildred and Martha	27
Brady Nicholas	28
Black Agnis	34

C	page no.
Coye Robert	3
Cotes Thomas	5
Cressey Thomas	16
<u>Idem</u> Thomas	16
Chossell Margaret	16
Clare Thomas	18
Curtis Robert	23
Corker William	24
Cressey Christofer	24
Chossell Margaret	25
Cobb John	26
Cornwallis Charles	28
Church William	32

D	page no.
Doughty Robert	8
Daye Joane	19
Durrant John	27

E	page no.
Eastow Francis	15
Empson Peeter	21
Empson Thomas	24
Elues John	28

GLOSSARY

AD OPUS ET USUM	To the work and use of.
AYLIENED	Transferred to the ownership of another (of property).
AMERCEMENT	A fine or fee in a manorial court.
APPURTENANCES	Minor properties.
ARMIGER	Esquire.
ASSIGNE	One to whom property or rights are transferred.
ASSIZE (ASSISE) RENTS	Fixed rents.
ATRIUM: ATREO: ATRIO	Entrance hall (Portico ?); central court of a Roman house.
BACKSIDE: BACKSCOE: BACKWAIE	Back premises; backyard (privy ?).
BAILIFF	One of the Lord of the manor's representatives, beneath the rank of Steward.
BAY	Division of space of building as defined by regular vertical features.
'BUILT UP'	With a building on it.
CABINA	Small room.
CARTBOTE	Old English name for right to take wood from the commons to make or repair carts.
CLERICUS	Churchman; scholar.
CLOSE	An enclosure from the open fields.
CONCLAVUM	Private room; closet.
COPYHOLD	Tenure of land by which the tenant was protected, not by national law, but by title written in Manor Court rolls.
COURT BARON	A manorial court which enforced the customs of the manor. It was presided over by the Lord or his steward and its main business was the care of and transfer of the Lord's lands. Its decisions were recorded in Court Rolls.

COURT LEET	A manorial court which was a court of record and public jurisdiction. It was presided over by the Lord or his steward.
CUM	With.
CURTILAGE	The yard and outbuildings of a house.
CUSTOMARY	According to the customs of the manor.
DEMESNE	Land retained by the Lord of the manor for his own use.
EDIFICIA PROMISSARE	A building planned, but not completed.
ENCLOSED	Land which had been enclosed from the open fields.
ESCHEATE	The reversion to the Lord, or the Crown, of an estate.
FEODARY	An officer concerned with the inheritance of land.
FEOFFEE	One of a board of trustees holding land for charitable or other public purposes.
FRANKPLEDGE	System by which every member of a tithing (group of ten men) was answerable for the good conduct of, or damage done by, any one of its members.
FREEHOLD	Free tenure, not subject to the custom of the manor or the will of the Lord. Its disposal after death was without restriction.
FURLONG	Originally a furrow length in an open field. Sometimes a measure of area, i.e. a rectangular block of strips.
FYERBOTE: FIREBOTE: FERBOTE	Old English name for the right to take wood from the commons for fuel.
GARDINO	Garden.
GAVELKIND	A custom by which a tenant's inheritance other than the widow's dower, which could be a half, was divided equally amongst his sons, or for want of sons amongst his daughters.
HEDGEBOTE	Old English term for the right to take wood from the commons to make and repair fences.
HERIOT(T)	The fee paid by an heir on entering into an estate.

HORR	Barn.
HORT (see ORT)	Garden.
HOWSEBOTE	Old English term for the right to take wood from the commons to make and repair houses.
INDENTURE	A deed or contract between parties.
LORD (of the MANOR)	See MANOR
MANOR	The land held by a Lord; e.g. Manor of Aylsham Lancaster. It could be a sub-division of a parish, or spread over two parishes. The various types of tenure (e.g. Copyhold, Freehold, Leasehold) allowed for a wide variety of customs, rights and obligations in each manor.
MESSUAGE	House and the ground around it.
OFFICINA	Outbuilding, domestic office.
OLLAND	Outland.
OPUS	Work.
ORT, ORTO (see also HORTO)	Garden.
PARCEL(L) (of land)	Piece (of land)
PERCH	A measure of length which could vary between 9ft and 26ft. Later standardised to 16½ feet.
PIGHTLE	A small field or enclosure.
PLOUGHBOTE	Old English term for the right to take wood from the common lands to make or repair ploughs.
RECTO	Right-hand page, or front of a leaf.
REEVE: REVE	A deputy - in a manor, or the tenant elected by fellow tenants to organise daily business of the manor.
RENTAL	Record of landholding.
ROD	Measure of length, same as PERCH.
ROOD	Measure of land corresponding to square perch: 40 square rods.
SENESCHAL	Steward.

SPAC	Bay (see BAY).
STADIO: STADIUM	Furlong.
STYE	Way.
SUIT(E)	The attendance which a tenant was obliged to give at the court of the Lord of the manor.
SURRENDER	The relinquishing of property to the Lord of the manor by a copyhold tenant.
TENEMENT	Land or real property held of another by any tenure; a dwelling place; residence.
TERRIER	A document giving legal and other information about landed property.
TOFT	A house, or the land where one has stood.
VERGATE: VIRGATE	A variable measure of land depending on soil quality; about 30 acres.
VERSO	Left-hand page, or back of a leaf.

ANALYSIS OF INFORMATION PROVIDED BY THE RENTAL

Some work has been done on the data which the Aylsham Rental provides: alphabetical lists of names, place names and topographical features have been prepared to facilitate further study. An analysis of the landholdings, aspects of inheritance, the transfer of property and the distribution of the transactions over the period of the rental has been undertaken, and the details are given on the following pages.

List of all the Names mentioned in the Aylsham Rental

List of Place Names and Topographical Features

Tenants in order of Rent, Land Value, and size of Landholding

In the following tables the tenants have been listed according to the amount of rent paid, the value of their land, and the size of their land-holding. When interpreting the findings it is important to remember that this Rental is for the manor of Lancaster, just one of four manors in Aylsham. The people listed here cannot be taken as representing the total number of land-holders in Aylsham, nor should the holding of any individual necessarily be taken as that person's entire land-holding.

With this reservation in mind, there are some interesting observations that can be made by comparing the three tables. The largest land-holder, whose land was also the most valuable, was Carolus Cornwallis, but he does not appear on the list of rent-payers: the reason for this invites further investigation. The mill was obviously a valuable asset, as reflected in the high rent paid by John Orwell. At the lower end of the scale there are large numbers of people paying the same rent, say 2d. or 1d., but they do not seem to relate to similar types or size of holding.

By studying the evidence provided by this rental, there are a great many questions that can be asked and, with further investigation, some of them can hopefully be answered.

Tenants in order of Rent

Name	Rent		
	£	s.	d.
John Orwell (Eliensis?)	8	12	10 (incl. mill)
Robert Wood and Anna	3	0	2½
Edward Brampton	1	19	2½
Gregory Breuiter	1	12	11¾
William Orwell (alone)	1	6	1½
Margaret Chosell	1	4	3
Simon Smyth (reeve)	1	3	10
William Orwell and Christiana	1	2	7
Thomas Larves		19	9
Francis Eastowe		19	8
Robert Doughty		19	3¼
John Jostehus		16	7½
James Smythe		15	1
Henry Some		14	4¾
Simon Leaverington		14	3
Thomas Smyth		14	1
Humphrey Holbye		13	5½
Richard Smith		12	0
Robert Baker		11	2¼
Mildren and Martha Baker		11	0
Thomas Norgate (gent.)		10	4
Thomas Coates		9	11
Robert Allyn		6	11
Robert Rumpe		6	11
Robert Bateman		6	9
Edmund Watts		6	8
John Some		6	6
Richard Bradye		6	1½
Thomas Cressy		5	11½
Thomas Hallifax		5	7
James Bell		5	4
Edward Allene		4	8
Robert Spendlove		4	6

Name	**Rent**		
	£	s.	d.
John Bradye		4	1½
Edmund Moulton		3	9
Launcelot Thexton		3	8
Thomas Munday (clericus)		3	5½
Thomas Allyn		3	1
William Kymer		2	8½
	+ some paid by father		
John Younges		2	7
Elizabeth Kymer		2	5½
John Pricke		2	4¾
William Baker		2	4
Thomas Knowles		2	4
John Haunde		2	2
John Barker		2	1
James Gedge (Hev.)		2	0
Robert Geagon, John Orwell, Robert Doughty + others		1	10½
James Gogle		1	10½
Robert Ventere (in right of his wife)		1	8
George Soute		1	7½
Thomas Empson		1	6
Rachel Norgate		1	6
Christopher Cressye		1	5½
Robert Rayner		1	4½
Margaret and John Furmery		1	2½
Thomas Edwards		1	1
John Warnes (Marsham)		1	0
Robert Gurney			11
William Woodrowe			10½
Edward Mayes			9½
Christopher Sankey			9½
William Scottow			9
Richard Wilson			8¼
Alice Godfrey			8
Edmund Haunde			8
William Kilby and Johanna			8
Thomas, Richard and James Smyth			7½

Name	**Rent** £ s. d.
Emma Smythe (widow)	$7\frac{1}{2}$
John Breuiter	$7\frac{1}{4}$ + some paid with Gregory Breuiter
William Lubbock (Scottow)	7
Robert Foster (alone)	6
Robert Foster and Margaret	6
William Harper	6
Robert Curtis	$5\frac{3}{4}$
Christopher Teylles	5
Robert Thompson	5
John Rymes (gent.) and Elizabeth	5
Gregory Whisoter	5
William Church	$4\frac{1}{2}$
Jacob Raymer	$4\frac{1}{2}$
Laurence Barr	4
Richard Tompson	4
Elizabeth Wadlowe	4
Henry Woodrow	4
William Corker	3
Katherine Scarboro	3
Johanna Ellis	$2\frac{1}{2}$
Johanna Akers	2
Agnes Aldridge	2
Agnes Black (Marsham)	2
Thomas Clare	2
William Greene	2
Alicia Homes	2
Agnes Horne (Marsham)	2
Edward Rye	2
William Tompson	2
Agneta Walker (Hev.)	2
Robert Bussell and Christiana	$1\frac{1}{2}$
Anna Thurston	$1\frac{1}{2}$
Robert Tompson	$1\frac{1}{2}$
Rowlande Turnor	$1\frac{1}{2}$

Name	Rent £	s.	d.
Nicholas Bradye			1
John Cobb			1
Robert Coye			1
Johanna Daye			1
Robert Gelle			1
William Moore			1
Alice Reymer			1
Robert and Richard Swanne			1
William Unipher			1
John Watson			1
Peter Welles			1
Edward Whitmore			1
John Jones			$\frac{3}{4}$
Thomas Harwood			$\frac{1}{2}$
Richard Thompson			$\frac{1}{2}$
John Warnes			$\frac{1}{2}$
Edmund Reve 'Seneschall'	pays no rent		
John Orwell jnr. John Barker jnr. Thomas Hallifax Simon Cressy and others } alms	rent paid by the grant		
John Breuiter	rent paid with Gregory Breuiter		

Rent not given

Carolus Cornwallis [largest land-holding]

John Durrant

Peter Empson

William Fisher

Robert Harmor

William Harmor

Johanna Haund

John Jostehus and Peter Barker

Thomas Leoman and Emma

Thomas Puttock

John Pye

Tenants in order of Land Value

Name		Value		
		£	s.	d.
Carolus Cornwallis		101	0	0
Robert Wood and wife Anna of Bolwick Manor		80	0	0
William Orwell and wife Christiana	£13 11 4)			
William Orwell	£37 6 4)	50	17	8
Edward Brampton		42	6	0
James Smythe		40	6	10
John Orwell (Eliensis)		28	6	8
Margaret Chosell		28	3	4
Thomas Leoman and wife Emma		28	2	4
Gregory Breviter		25	0	0
Richard Smith		22	2	8
Peter Barker and John Jostehus		20	6	8
Mildred and Martha Baker		19	16	8
Thomas Smyth		19	13	4
Robert Doughty Gent.		18	5	4
Francis Eastowe (woman)		17	12	0
Thomas Coates		16	8	4
Thomas Norgate Gent.		16	0	0
Thomas Lawes		14	4	6
John Breviter		13	6	9
Humphrey Holbye		12	13	10
William Kymer		11	17	0
Thomas Cressy		11	15	2
Edward Allene		10	18	0
Simon Leaverington		10	12	2
Thomas Munday Clericus		10	5	0
Edmund Reve		10	0	0
John Bradye		8	9	4
Robert Baker		8	8	0
Robert Allyn		8	6	8
Thomas Puttock		8	6	8
Robert Rumpe		8	0	0
Robert Bateman		7	16	9

Name	Value		
	£	s.	d.
Edmund Watts	7	16	0
John Barker	6	14	4
James Bell	6	8	4
William Baker	5	17	4
Launcelot Thexton	4	17	8
Robert Ventere	4	13	4
George Soute	3	6	0
Thomas Knowles	2	12	0
John Younges	2	10	0
NIcholas Bradye	2	10	0
Thomas Gedge (Heavingham)	2	5	0
John Haunde	2	0	0
Elizabeth Kymer	1	13	4
Henry Woodrow	1	10	6
Robert Geagon Advocate, and others 'Le Schoolhouse'	1	10	4
William Scottow	1	6	8
Robert Foster and wife Margaret	1	4	0
Edmund Haunde	1	2	0
John Rymes Gent.	1	0	0
John Cobb	1	0	0
Edward Mayes	1	0	0
James Gogle with James Smyth	1	0	0
William Woodrowe (Skeyton)		18	0
Robert Curtis		16	0
Thomas Allen (Marsham)		15	0
Robert Gurney		14	4
Johanna Daye		13	4
Robert Thompson		13	4
John Jones		12	0
Thomas Clare		12	0
Alice Godfrey		11	0
Rachel Norgate		11	0
William Church (Skeyton)		11	0
Gregory Whissiter		11	0
John Pricke		10	8
Christopher Teylles		10	0

Name	Value		
	£	s.	d.
William Kilby and wife Johanna		10	0
William Tompson		10	0
Alicia Homes		8	8
John Pye		8	6
Thomas Empson		8	0
William Greene		8	0
James Gogle		7	6
Laurence Burr		7	4
Edward Whitmore		6	8
William Corker		6	8
Katherine Scarboro		6	8
Johanna Akers		6	0
William Fisher		6	0
William Harper		6	0
Em[m]a Smythe		6	0
Anna Thurston		6	0
Robert Rayner		5	6
Johanna Elles		5	0
Rowlande Turner		5	0
Robert Harmer		4	0
John Some		4	0
John Watson		4	0
Margaret and John Furmery (Vicar of Aylsham)		3	4
William Unipher		3	4
Richard Thompson		3	4
Alice Reymer		3	4
Robert Thompson		3	4
Peter Empson		3	4
Jacob Rayner		3	0
Agnes Aldridge		2	6
William Moore		2	6
Robert Coye		2	6
Edward Rye		2	2
Agnes Walker (Heavingham)		2	0
Robert Gelle		1	8

No value recorded

Agnes Black	(Marsham)	by charter
Thomas Edwards	(Scottow)	
Agnes Horne	(Marsham)	freehold by charter
William Lubbock	(Scottow)	by charter

Edmund Moulton and wife Dorothy (Scottow)

Tenants in order of size of Landholding

Name	**Total Landholding**			
Carolus Cornwallis	236 ac			
Robert Wood and Anna	174½ ac	4½ rood		
Edward Brampton	149½ ac	14 rood	37 perch	
James Smythe	136½ ac	2½ rood		15ft stall
William Orwell (alone)	116 ac	8½ rood		
Simon Smyth (reeve)	104½ ac	1 rood		8ft x 4ft stall
Margaret Chosell	93 ac	19 rood	51 perch	284ft
Richard Smith	88 ac			
Gregory Breuiter	65 ac			
Thomas Leoman and Emma	64½ ac	15 rood		9 yds
Mildred and Martha Baker	62 ac	2 rood	6 perch	
Thomas Smyth	62 ac		10 perch	
Robert Doughty	60 ac	2½ rood		
John Orwell (Eliensis)	57 ac	2 rood	20 perch +	mill
Francis Eastowe	56 ac			
Henry Some	55 ac	3 rood		
Thomas Norgate (Gent.)	53 ac	7½ rood		26 virgate(?
Thomas Coates	51½ ac	11 rood		
Humphrey Holbye	44 ac	10½ rood	20 perch	stall + shop
William Orwell and Christiana	41 ac	8½ rood		51 yds
John Breuiter	41 ac			
John Jostehus and Peter Barker	39½ ac	4½ rood	12 perch	
Thomas Puttock	38½ ac	15 rood	8 perch	
Thomas Larves	34 ac	1 rood		
Edward Allene	30 ac	1 rood		10ft
Robert Baker	28 ac			
Thomas Cressy	27 ac	17 rood		
John Some	27 ac	1 rood		
Simon Leaverington	26½ ac	6½ rood	27 perch	12ft x 2 perch
Thomas Munday (Clericus)	25 ac	½ rood		
William Kymer	18½ ac	8 rood	16 perch	
Robert Bateman	17½ ac	6 rood		
James Bell	17 ac			

Name	Total Landholding		
Edmund Watts	16 ac	3½ rood	
Robert Bussell and Christiana	16 ac	1 rood	6 perch
Robert Allyn	16 ac		
John Barker	15 ac	2 rood	
Robert Ventere - in right of his wife	13½ ac		
Edmund Reve (seneschall)	13 ac	10 rood	
Robert Rumpe	13 ac		
Thomas Knowles	12 ac		
Launcelott Thexton	10½ ac	2½ rood	
Richard Bradye	10 ac		
John Bradye	9 ac	10 rood	
John Younges	7 ac	5 rood	
Thomas Allyn	7 ac	1 rood	8 perch
Edmund Moulton	7 ac	½ rood	
George Soute	6½ ac	4 rood	
Thomas Harwood	5½ ac	3 rood	
Christopher Cressye	5½ ac	1 rood	
James Gedge (Hev.)	5½ ac	1 rood	
William Baker	5 ac		8 perch
John Haunde	5 ac		
Richard Wilson	4 ac	7½ rood	
Robert Curtis	4 ac		
Edmund Haunde	4 ac		
William Scottow	3½ ac	3 rood	3 perch
William Woodrowe	3 ac		
Elizabeth Kymer	2½ ac		+ tenement shop
Edward Mayes	2½ ac		
Christopher Teylles	2½ ac		
William Church	2 ac	3 rood	
William Lubbock (Scottow)	2 ac	3 rood	
John Cobb	2 ac		
Robert Foster (alone)	2 ac		
Robert Foster and Margaret	2 ac		
Robert Geagon, John Orwell, Robert Doughty and others	2 ac		
John Rymes (Gent.) and Elizabeth	2 ac		
Robert Spendlove	2 ac		

Name	Total Landholding			
John Warnes (Marsham)	2 ac			
Gregory Whissoter	1½ ac			2 stalls
Richard Tompson	1 ac	4 rood		
Agnes Black (Marsham)	1 ac			
Robert Gelle	1 ac			
Agnes Horne (Marsham)	1 ac			
Thomas Edwards	½ ac	4 rood		
Thomas Hallifax	½ ac	2 rood	20 perch	2 spac
Thomas Empson	½ ac			
Robert Thompson	½ ac			
Thomas, Richard and James Smyth		7 rood		
Emma Smythe		7 rood		
Laurence Barr		4 rood		
Robert Gurney		4 rood		
Nicholas Bradye		3 rood		
William Greene		3 rood		
William Kilby and Johanna		3 rood		
Johanna Daye		2 rood		
John Pye		2 rood		
Agueta Walker (Hev.)		2 rood		
John Warnes		2 rood		
James Gogle		1½ rood	4 perch	18ft x 5ft
Henry Woodrow		1 rood	12 perch	11ft
John Pricke		1 rood		
Robert and Richard Swanne		1 rood		
William Thompson		1 rood		
Johanna Haund		½ rood		
Anna Thurston		½ rood		
Peter Welles		½ rood		
Johanna Ellis			32 perch	
Rachel Norgate			30 perch	
William Fisher			22 perch	
Rowlande Turnor			20 perch	
Elizabeth Wadlowe			13 perch	
Jacob Rayner			10 perch x 2 perch	
Margaret and John Furmery			10 perch	
William Harper			10 perch	

Name	Total Landholding
Robert Tompson	10 perch
John Watson	10 perch
Alicia Homes	8 perch
Richard Thompson	7 perch
Johanna Akers	4 perch
Alice Reymer	4 perch
Christopher Sankey	3 perch + shop + stalls
Robert Coye	2 perch
John Durrant	2 perch
John Jones	70ft
William Harmor	30ft sq. stall
Alice Godfrey	20ft
Edward Rye	20ft
Robert Raymer	18ft x 6ft and 18ft x 1ft
William Corker	15ft x 12ft
William Moore	12ft
Edward Whitmore	10ft sq.
Robert Harmor	7ft x 4ft stall
William Unipher	stall 7ft circumference
No size given	
Agnes Aldridge	stall
Thomas Clare	tenement
Peter Empson	part of shop
Katherine Scarboro	tenement

Alms: paid by the grant

John Orwell jnr.

John Barker jnr.

Thomas Holifax

Simon Cressy and others

Inheritance and Landholding Patterns

Although the usual pattern of inherited property ownership was from father to son, a surprising number of properties in this rental are owned by women - indeed some women were major property owners (vide Margaret Chosell). Others owned property in their own right aside from their joint ownership of other holdings (vide Martha Baker). Perhaps this reflects the practice of 'gavelkind' in this manor (see MSS page 38). We have included a list of married couples and 'partners' holding land, and a list of properties inherited through the maternal line. In a few cases men held properties in the right of their wives or children.

Inheritance other than from father to son

	Page no.
Gelle, Robert to William Brook	23
Holmes, Alicia to son	20
Horne, Agnes to son	34
Leoman, Emma from mother	22
Norgate, Rachel to sons	22v
Norgate, Thomas from mother	25
Orwell, Christiana to son John Barker	14v

Total: 7

Siblings/partners holding jointly

Baker, Mildred and Martha	27
Furmery, Margaret and John	28
Geagon, Robert; Orwell, John and Doughty, Robert	17v
Gogle, James and Smyth, James	4
Justehus, John and Barker, Peter	14v
Neave, William and Leoman, Thomas	35
Norgate, Henry and Edward	25
Orwell, John Jr; Barker, John Jr; Halifax, Thomas and Cressy, Simon	17v
Pettus, Edward and George	29
Rightwaies, Johanna and Burrowe, Johanna	17
Smyth, Thomas, Richard and James	27
Swanne, Robert and Richard	10

Total: 12

Women holding land

	Page no.
Akers, Johanna	20
Aldridge, Agnes	1
Baker, Mildred and Martha	27
Black, Agnes	34
Chosell, Margaret	16v, 17, 17v, 25v
Daye, Johanna	19
Eastowe, Francis	15
Elles, Johanna	28
Godfrey, Alice	26v
Haund, Johanna	27v
Homes, Alicia	20
Horne, Agnes	34
Kymer, Elizabeth	19v, 20
Norgate, Rachel	22v
Reymer, Alice	22v
Scarboro Katherina	1
Smythe, Emma	22v
Thurston, Anna	28
Wadlowe, Elizabeth	23
Waller, Agnes	33

Total: 20

Men holding in right of wives/children

	Page no.
Foster (Margaret and Robert) for sons	26v
Gurney, Robert for wife	11
Holbye, Humphrey for wife	7
Orwell, William for wife	14v
Sankey, Christopher for wife	9
Ventere, Robert for wife	22v

Total: 6

Married couples holding land

Allyn (Robert and Elizabeth)	3
Baker (Robert and Martha)	8
Bell (James and Elizabeth)	2
Bussell (Robert and Christiana)	24, 24v
Foster (Robert and Margaret)	26v
Kilby (William and Johanna)	26v
Leoman (Thomas and Emma)	21v
Moulton (Edmund and Dorothy)	31v
Orwell (William and Christiana)	13
Rymer (John and Elizabeth)	15
Smythe (James and Johanna)	10v
Watts (Edmund and Susanna)	5
Welles (Peter and Dorothy)	31v
Wood (Robert and Anna)	20v

Total: 14

ASSOCIATED DOCUMENTS

The rental is primarily a list of landholdings compiled about 1625. Its compiler was not concerned to record other information about individual tenants. In a few cases their position or professional qualification is mentioned: Edward Reve is the Steward of the Manor; Thomas Munday is 'clericus'; Robert Geogan is 'armiger' ; Simon Smith and John Orwell are described as bailiffs. Market stall holders and shop owners are named. To learn more about the private and domestic lives of these tenants it is necessary to turn to other sources of information. One such source is the wills made by the tenants and proved in the ecclesiastical courts of the time, along with the inventories of their property made at the time of their death. Both sets of documents are now stored in the Norfolk Record Office. In a preliminary survey of the tenants six were found who had both wills and inventories surviving; one of these, selected at random, is included here as a sample of what can be learnt about life in a community such as Aylsham at this time.

We learn that Edmund Watts was a baker with a wife and six children at the time of his death. In the rental he holds 16 acres, the fourteenth largest holding. Yet in his will he bequeaths much more than this to his family. Presumably the remainder was in another manor or elsewhere in the county and he was a wealthier citizen than might be supposed from the information supplied by the rental alone.

Will of Edmund Watts, Baker of Aylsham 1639

Edmund Wattes **NCC Wills 1639 (174 Green) MF412**

In the name of God Amen

The twenty day of February Anno Domi 1639. I Edmond Wattes of Aylesum in the County of Norf: Baker doe make and ordaine this my last Will & Testament in manner & form Following. First I Commend my Soule into the mercifull hands of Allmighty God hoping Assurerly to be saved by the Meritts & Mercy of Christ Jesus my onely Saviour & Redeemer & I Commend my Body to the Earth from whence it com. **Item** I give unto Elizabeth Wattes my Daughter one Close caled the gravellpitt Close: Situated and being in Aylesum aforesaid conteyning together seaven Acres of lands being more or less Sometime Henry Holbeys to the use of the same Elizabeth Wattes & her Heirs immediatly after my Deseace. **Item** I will and my mind is that Susan Wattes my wife shall have the use and Occupation of all other my Houses, Lands & Tenements situated & being in Aylesum aforesaid During her naturall Life the Remainder whereof to be to such use & uses As herein are to be Nominated.

Item I will that the said Susann my wife Shall keep all ye Houses in good & sufficient Repairations not doing or suffering any strop or wast to be made or done upon the premisses. **Item** I will and my minde is that After the Deseace of Susann my wife that Jeames Wattes my sonn shall have all those Houses, Orchards and Lands with Appurtenences scituate & being in Stongate in Aylesum aforesaid. (the gravelpitt Close excepted) Conteining together by estimation eighteen acres of land being more or less now in the occupation of Thomas Pricke to the use of the said Jeames Wattes my sonn And his Heirs , upon Condition notwithstanding That The said Jeames Watts my sonn his Heirs Executors, or Assinges shall pay or cause to be payd unto Susann Watts my Daughter or Assings Thirty pounds of lawfull money of England in manner & forme following that is to say Tenn pounds within one Year next after my Deseace Tenn pounds within two Years next after my Deseace &

Tenn pounds in full payment & satisfaction of the said thirty pounds within three Years next after my Deseace at or within the South porch of the parish Church of Aylesum aforesaid. **Provided** that if the said Jeames Wattes my sonn his Heires or Assinges shall refuse & make Default of payment of the said Thirty pounds in manner & form as is aforesaid. **Item** I will the said Houses, Orchards & Lands with the Appurtenences as is aforesaid to be to the use of the said Susann,& her heirs, immediatly after the Deseace of the said Susann my wife. **Item** I give unto Richard Wattes my sonn all that my Messuages with the Barnes,Stables,Yards,Orchards,& Gardens with the Appurtenences wherein I now Dwell sometime Knolls & Eighteen Acres of Land being more or less Caled Golsternes six Acres of Lands inclosed being Furground sometime Chapmans To Have and to Hold all the said messuage with the Appurtenences The Eighteen Acres of Land caled Golsternes the Six Acres of Fur round called Chapmans to use of the said Richard Watts my sonn his Heirs ['& Assinges' crossed out] immediately after the Deseace of the said Susann my wife uppon Condition that the said Richard Wattes my sonn his Heirs or Assinges, shall pay or cause to be payd to the William Wattes my sonn or to his Assinges one Hundred pounds of Lawfull money of England in manner And forme following that is to say fifty pounds with one yeare next after the Deseace of Susann my wife & fifty pounds in full payment & satisfaction of the said one Hundred pounds within two years next after the Deseace of the said Susann my wife at or within the South porch of the parrish Church of Aylesum Aforesaid Provided if the said Richard my sonn shall refuse or make default of payment of the said one Hundred pounds in manner & forme as aforesaid. Then I will the said Eighteen Acres of Land Caled Golsternes to be to the use of the said William Wattes & his Heires forever.

Edmond Wattes

Witnesses, Eusebius Harvy: William Kilbye: Christopher Cressy; Rowland Tirwer [Turner]:

Provided further my Will and my Mind is that whereas I have given all my lands & tenements to Susann my wife during her naturall life that the said Susann my wife shall pay yearly to the Richard my Sonn Six pounds of Lawfull money of England during the naturall life of the said Susann which if the said Susann shall refuse to perform as is aforesaid, then I will the said Richard my sonn shall enter into all the said Houses, Lands & Tenements to him in this my last will immediately upon the Deniell of the said Six pounds or parte thereof the beging [sic] the first payment which to beging [sic] at his age of one and twenty years. **Item** I give unto Susann Wattes my wife & to her Heirs immediately after Deseace fower Acres of Land inclosed Caled Thurstenes Close lying in Aylesum aforesaid and one Meadow lying in Blickling in the County of Norff: to the intent that she the said Susann my wife shall pay my Debts and also to pay unto Ales Wattes my Daughter twenty pounds of money of England in manner & form following: **Viz** tenn pounds within one year next after my Deseace and tenn pounds within two years next after my Deseace And that the said Susann my wife shall release all her Right & Tythe of Donerof in the gravell pitt Close to the use of Elizabeth my Daughter uppon Lawfull Demand. **Item** I give unto Poore People of Aylesum forty shillings. **Item** I give unto William Wilson of London Fishmonger five pounds to be payd to him within half year next after my Deseace by my Executrix. **Item** I give William Prick my GrandChild five pounds to be payd to him at his Age of fifteen years. **Item** I give Love Bernard xx s [20s]. All other my goods, Chattels, moveables, & implements of Household Stuffe I give them to Susann my wife whom I make sole Executrix of this my last Will and Testament to the better inabling her to pay all my Debts, Legacies And to see my Body Decently brought to Chritian Buriall. And this I publish & acknowledge to be my last will, Revoking all former Wills in Witness whereof I have sett my hand & seale: the Day and year first above written
Edmond Watts.

Witnesses, Eusebius Harvy: William Kilbye: Rowland Tirwer [Turner]; Christopher Cressy:

Inventory of the Property of Edmund Watts 1639

Edmund Wattes INV 45/267

A true Inventorie made the third Daye of Marche, Anno Domini 1639 of all the goodes, Chattles Cattles,moveables and implementes of householde stuffe which wer Edmund Wattes of Aylesham in the Countie of Norffolk Baker, late deceasede seene and prysed by us whose names ar here underwitten viz

[blank]

Imprimis in the parlor, one bedsted	ij^{li}	x^{s}
Item one fetherbed. j fether bolster. j pillowe one rugg koverlet		
fyve kurtans, with thre kurtane roddes with Cord and matt	$iiij^{li}$	
Item one liverie kobberd as it stand		xx^{s}
Item one table one forme two chaires one carpet. vj kuchins one truncke		xlv^{s}
Item one loking glasse, one paire of bellowes one paire of dogyrones.		
one barr of yron, one hake		xx^{s}
Item the plate	$xviij^{li}$	
Item in the little parlor, one bedstead as it stande	$iiij^{li}$	
Item two tables, one chaire, two strooles, one paire of dog irones		xx^{s}
Item in the buttrie, one meatfill, one salting keeler with [crossed out]		
one charne, one halfe barrell with pottes and glasses and other provigion		xl^{s}
Item in the hall, one kobberd & cobberdis bothe, one table one forme, two		
chestes one liverie koberd, one trunke, one little boxe, one stoole	iij^{li}	x^{s}
Item the bookes		xx^{s}

Item	li	s	d
Item in the kitchin, one kewle, one keepe one table, fowre buffet stooles, viij chaires		xl^{s}	
Item the pewter	iij^{li}	x^{s}	
Item the brasse	iij^{li}		
Item one warming pan, two drippin pans iiij spytes one [crossed out] two morteres, one chafin dishe two brasse kandlestickes, with other implementes as dogg yrons, fyre pan tonges, bellowes a barr of yron and hakes	$iiij^{li}$		
Item one musket furnished		xl^{s}	
Item in the bakehouse one braye, one trowghe ij moulding bordes with the peetes skales and weightes		xx^{s}	
Item one brandlet one paire of doggyrones ij hakes with other necessarie thinges in the backhouse		x^{s}	
Item in the bruehouse one smale kopper with the brueing vesseles & other tubbes		xl^{s}	
Item in the bulting chamber one bulthyn [?] hutche, with other lumber		xx^{s}	
Item in the corne chamber xiiij combes of whete	x^{li}		
Item fyve combes barlye		$xxxiij^{s}$	$iiij^{d}$
Item the kreene fan and bushell		$xxvj^{s}$	$viij^{d}$
Item in the kitchin chamber, one bedstede one trendlebed two liverie bedes fower fetherbedes six fether bolsteres fower pillowes two rugges two koverlettes, thre blankettes	$xiij^{li}$		
Item one chest one table, one closestool one forme		x^{s}	
Item in the barne, iiij combz Rye in the strawe and fowre combz barlie in the strawe	iij^{li}	vj^{s}	$viij^{d}$

Item the strawe		x^{s}	
Item in the stable, j nagg & one mare	iiij^{li}		
Item the furniture for husbandrie		xiij^{s}	iiij^{d}
Item ij loades of haye		xx^{s}	
Item two mylche kowes	vj^{li}		
Item iij swyne		xx^{s}	
Item in the fuw barne one carte		xx^{s}	
Item the Fytches and the chaffe		x^{s}	
Item the plowe and the harrowes		xx^{s}	
Item the woode in the yarde the Furres and the muck		xxx^{s}	
Item the grayne growing of fowre acres of lande	vij^{li}		
Item one diapre bordeclothe vj diapre napkins and thre kobberde clothes		xxx^{s}	
Item two paire of hollandde sheetes j dozen of table napkins and xj paire of ordinarie sheetes	vj^{li}		
Item in other lynnen smale and gret		xxv^{s}	
Item his apparrell	v^{li}		
Item thinges negligentlie forgotten		v^{s}	

Summa totall 127^{li} 5^{s}

[Signatures] William Kilbye
his merke
Henrey Holbey
Thomas Pricke
Xtofer Cressy

OTHER CONTEMPORARY DOCUMENTS

From the Aylsham Rental it has been possible to learn much about the circumstances and way of life of seventeenth-century Aylsham people. There are however other contemporary documents which, used in conjunction with the Rental, can give its data a wider perspective. Three have been selected for this purpose and transcriptions of them have been made and are included here. Others, as mentioned in the Introduction, would be a rewarding further study.

Dispute with the Queen, 1600 (see pp. 132-135)

In the Rental one of the maps (see cover) depicts an area of heathland - Stonegate Heath - lying between Aylsham and Cawston then called Meadow Hyrne or the King's Common Ground, the ownership of which was in dispute between the men of Aylsham and the men of Cawston. The following document, dated 1600, is the outcome of an earlier dispute about the same stretch of heathland, this time between Queen Elizabeth and the tenants of Aylsham about common rights. The Duchy Court of Lancaster finds in favour of the tenants, allowing the Queen only the sweepage, i.e. the hay crop!

Demands of the Tenants of Aylsham, 1641 (see pp. 136-138)

In 1631 Sir John Hobart of Blickling finally purchased the freehold of the Manor of Lancaster (see page 8 of the Introduction). It appears that the tenants of Aylsham felt that he, as their landlord, was taking away some of their ancient rights and customs and exacting more in fines than was justifiable. They therefore prepared the following document stating their complaints. In the margin on the left the agreements finally reached are recorded.

Description of Tenement in Aylsham called Netherhall, 1620 (see p. 139)

This glebe terrier - a record of church property - describes a tenement called Netherhall adjoining Netherhall Street in 1620. Which street this was is not known, but it must have been close to the church and the vicarage of the period. In the Rental a Katherine Scarboro is recorded (see page 19) as having a tenement in Netherhall Street but there is no direct evidence to identify it with this one.

Dispute with the Queen, 1600

19th April 1600

Copy

Exemplification of a Decree in the Dutchy Court of Lancaster that 60 acres of Furze Bruery[1] and More in Aylsham is Commonable by the Copyhold Tenants & the Crown intitled only to the Sweepage

Elizabeth by the Grace of God Queen of England France and Ireland Defender of the faith etc. to all men to whom these present letters shall come greetings. **We have Inspected** the tenor of certain Orders and Decrees in the Chamber of our Duke of Lancaster at Westminster amongst the Records of the said Duke there remaining and existing in these Words **In the Easter Term** the forty-second year of the reign of Queen Elizabeth on Saturday the nineteenth of April 1600 Between the said Queen, and Firman Lawes, John Some, Simon Smythe and Henry Coates Defendants. **This** Daye the cause dependinge in this Courte betweene her Majestie and the sayd Defendants was fully heard in open Courte and att large debated by Counsell learned as well on the parte of her Majestye as on the parte and behalf of the sayd Defendants before Mister Baron Clarke and other her Majesties Commissions of this Courte for and concerninge a parcell of Firreground Bruerye and Moore lyinge in Aylsham in the County of Norfolk contayneinge by Estimacion Sixe Score Acres or therabouts Claymed by her Highnes in an Informacion on her behalf there exhibyted by her Majesties Attorney of the same Courte against the sayde Defendants to bee her Severall Inherytance and parcell of her Highnes Mannor of Aylesham and pretended to bee called by the name of the Queenes Severall also Meadowe hyrne and alsoe alledged to have been heretofore letten or demysed by her Majestie under the Seale of her Duchie of Lancaster for dyverse Yeares now past, which sayde whole

1. Heath

peece of Fyrregrounde Bruerye and Moore ys by the Defendants in their Annsweares confessed to bee her Majesties Soyle and Freehold and parcell of her sayd Mannor of Aylesham but not called by the name of the Queenes Severall albeyt they doo confesse that parte of the east end thereof ys called by the name of Meadowe hyrne, But they the sayd Defendants doo alledge and saye upon their oathe in their sayd Annsweare that parte of the sayd peece of Fyrregrounde Bruerye and Moore hath bene tyme out of Mynd of Man demysed and Demysable by Copye of Court Roll of the said Mannor according to the Custome of the sayd Mannor which are and have bene accordingly holden and enjoyed by the sayd Defendants and others to this daye, And that the Residue of the sayd Sixe score Acres which ys not soe holden which amounts by Estimation to threescore Acres or therabouts ys and tyme out of Mynd hath bene called by the name of Stonegate Heathe also the Queenes Common. And therin the sayde Defendants for themselves and some other of her Majesties Tenants of the sayd Mannor dwellinge in Stonegate and Woodgate Streete in Aylesham aforesayd by their sayd Annsweare clayme Common of Pasture as belonginge to their Tenements in Aylsham which they Severallye hould of the sayd Mannor for all their Cattle Commonable Levant & Couchante uppon their Severall Tenements aforesayd granntinge neverthelesse that her Majestie and her Progenitors have had and ought to have the Sweepage of the said Threescore Acres by Estimacion not holden by Copye as aforesayd **Nowe** for as much as uppon the hearinge of the sayde Cause yt appeares playnly by very many anncyent Wyttnesses that the sayd Defendants and some other of her Majesties Tenants as namely Robert Skiffynne and Ralphe Archer and those whose Estate they have for these Threescore and tenn Yeares and downewards to this day have had the Feede thereof which all their greate Cattell Levant & Couchant uppon their sayd Tenements and by anncyent Accompts of the tymes of Henry the Sixt Henry the Seaventh Henry the Eight and the Queene that now ys that the sayd Kings and

and Queene had beene annsweared by the Bayliffs of the sayd Mannor Sometymes Fower Shillings sometymes more and sometymes less for the Fengerye and Bruerye uppon the Common of Aylsham being the place in Questyon, And that Surchargyes and wrongfull Commons had beene lykewyse punnished there by the name of a Common which proved that of Anntiquitye yt had bene called and reputed Common other then for the Sweepage And thoughe yt were proved on the other syde by one Thomas Orwell that one Christmas had taken a lease of the Mannor of Aylsham and had by reason thereof demysed the sayd grounde in Questyon and that one Iveson had since taken an other lease of the same peece by ytself and that the Townesmen of Aylsham had geven to Christmas Threescore poundes for his said Lease and to Iveson five pounds five Shillings and Eight pence yet the same beinge annsweared that the Threescore pounds was geven for the Lease of the Mannor beinge beneficiall for the Tenants and that the five poundes Sixe Shillings and Eight pence was gyven to Iveson at the Request of Sir Christopher Heydon as towards his Chardges and because yt appeared not to the Courte that any Rent had ever beene annsweared for the same to her Majestie uppon the sayd Leases nor any possession thereby had but the contrarye thereof playnlye deposed namelye that the Tenants contynued their use of Feede there as before in right of their sayd Commonage **Therefore** this Courte doth **Order and Decree** that as well the sayd Defendants John Some Fyrmyne Lawes Symon Smythe and Henry Coates as alsoe the said Robert Skyphnne and Ralphe Archer their Heyres and Assygnes Occupyors of their sayd Messuages and Tenementes in Stonegate or Woodgate Streete in Aylsham aforesayd shall in respect of their saide Copyehold Estates in their Severall Tenementes aforesayd have and take such Common of pasture in and uppon the aforesayd Resydue of the sayde peece of Firre grounde Bruerye and Moore which ys not holden by Copye as aforesayd for all their great Cattell Levant and Cowchant uppon their sayd Customary Tenements and in such manner and Forme as they and their Assignes Tenants thereof have heretofore had and used to have and take in and uppon the same And as touchinge the Firres Whynnes Linge brakes Turfes [?]aggs Thornes and other Sweepage yearlye groweinge uppon the sayd Heathe or Bruerye which ys not Customarye hold. **It ys allsoe Ordered and Decreed** by this Courte that the same shall be had and taken to her Majesties use and bee bestowed in such Sorte as heretofore yt hath bene without any Clayme or Challenge therunto to bee had or made by these Defendants or any of them their Fermers or Assignes and to bee sold by her Majesties Fermors of the sayde Bruerye or the Bayliffe of the sayde Mannor for the tyme being for and to her Majesties best benefytt and avayle savinge that this Courte doth think fitt that her Majesties sayd Tenants that have Common of pasture uppon the sayd Heathe shall have the preferrment thereof before any Stranger **We therefore by the Tenor** of the aforesaid Ordinances and Decrees at the Instance and the Requisition [Suit of Court] of the aforesaid Defendants we have conveyed an exemplification of these presents (this document] **In witness whereof** these are letters patent we have made **Given** at our palace of Westminster under the Seal of our Duchy of Lancaster aforesaid the fifth day of May in the forty-second year of our Reign.

Gerrard. [signed]

27 March 1641	The demandes of the Tenants of Aylesham
	That the rolls be constantly kept in the Towne Chest as formerly
	That the Tenants be termed customarie Tenants as formerly
	That no Tenant be amerced above iij^{d} for default of suite of Court
	That they maye fell and sell timber & decaye houses at thier pleasure
With fitt cautions	That they maye lease thier landes & tenementes for 21 yeares without lycence
agreed unto	
2^{s} on the one side	That they paye but xij^{d} an acre fine & xij^{d} a messuage tenement, & cotage
xj^{s} on the other side	in fee simple
or xviij^{d} generally	and for shopps and stalls xj^{d}
agreed unto.	and for life halfe so much
	and for Guardians for Infants a quarter so much
to be reduced to a	and mortgage without fine untill admittance.
certen time agreed unto	
all arbitrarie fines	That all fines formerly paide be reduced to these paymentes
heretofore [paide, crossed	and the one plus repaide to the severall persons respectively
out] receiued to be reduced	as allso arbitrarie heriots
to the fines agreed	
by the Indenture	That they maye plant trees upon the wastes of the manner agaynst thier owne
agreed unto.	houses & groundes, & to take them of, & conuert them to thier owne use.

Sir John desires time to consider of this, but conceiues it to be no waye reasonable If the Tenants refuse this, Sir John offereth to referre it to anye indifferent men. The Tenants are content to referre this.

If these agreements proceede Sir John desires that the rentes maye be [gathered, crossed out] collected by the Tennantes as Heywardes accordinge to the ancient custome

The Tennants are content to collect the rentes, & desire Sir John wilbe pleased to giue the Collector the profittes of

That all new grantes be confirmed

That all such as haue not formerly paide thier thirtie yeares purchase may paye the same, & that to be distributed amonge such whose moneys are spent in the suites.

That all such as haue formerly paide maye come in without further payment.

That the manner be confirmed to Sir John Hobart & his heires

That those customes be confirmed to the Tennants & that by act of Parliament

That Sir John Hobart wilbe pleased to [condiscende, crossed out] to keepe the Market crosse in repaire, seeinge he take the profitt of the Fayre & market.

These we doe humbly desire Sir John Hobart wilbe pleased to condiscende unto, & that he will forgett all by past business, & we will both honour him & praye for him:

They whose names are under written doe agree hereunto.

Thomas Knolles	Martha Smith	Symon Leuerinhton
Thomas Leman	John Bradie	Thomas Lawes

the Fayre & markett, & they will
maynteyne the market Crosse.

Robert Doughtie	Henry Soame	John Hawnde
Peter Empson	Henry Rogerson	Henry Holbye
Christopher Sankey	Thomas Cressye	Francis Bell
Richard Andrewes	John Durrant	Thomas Allines
Rowland Turner	Robert Curties	John Ellys
Katharine Swift	John Smith	Gregory Wisseter
Margaret Allines	Thomas Smith	
Alice Allines	Mildred Smith	
John Neaue. miller	John Cobbe	

Description of Tenement in Aylsham called Netherhall, 1620   NRO NRS 12921 27E7

A Coppy of the terrier delyvered unto the Dean & Chapter of Canterbery 1620

[Top of document damaged]
[Three words missing] terrier of the Rectory or parsonage of Aylesham in the County of Norfolk the tenth daye of October 1620.

The tenement called Netherhall Viz A Hall parler kitchin pantry seller milking house backhause and Maulting house adioyninge upon a streete called Netherhall street est of the sayd tenement two bearnes two outhouses the yardes and groundes adioyninge upon the tenement contayninge by estimation fouer Acres and doth abut south upon the viccaridge of Aylesham and north upon the tenement and grounds late John Clares now in the tenure and occupation of Thomas Knowles and lieth west upon the kinges highe waye out

Henry Croft
Robert Sier

MAP - THE POSITION OF AYLSHAM

Aylsham lies almost midway between Norwich and the coast. Cromer, or its predecessor Shipden, provided a small port from which goods could be exported or through which Newcastle coals, Scandinavian timber or iron could be imported. Aylsham also lies at a crossroads where the Dereham road crosses the Norwich-Cromer road; this road, now the B1145, once led to the famous shrine at Bromholm Abbey in Bacton on the coast where part of the holy cross was preserved. Until the dissolution of the monasteries Bromholm was visited by kings and queens and was the burial place of the famous, such as John Paston in 1466. Several market towns lay on this west to east route, of which Aylsham was one.

The market in Aylsham was first recorded in the reign of King Edward I in 1296; it lay, as it still does, on the plateau to the south of the valley of the River Bure. The river, flowing between its broad valley sides from its main source near Melton Constable down through Saxthorpe/Corpusty, Itteringham and Ingworth, meanders through rich meadows on a wide flood plain past Aylsham and down through Buxton/Lamas, Coltishall/Horstead to become part of the Broadland system there. It has provided a good head of water to power the water wheels at Aylsham Mill since at least 1086 when a mill was recorded in Domesday Book.

The existing beautiful parish church was not built until the fourteenth century but there must have been a smaller church on that site for perhaps three hundred years before that. Much of the rebuilding of the church is attributed to John of Gaunt (1340-1399), the son of Edward III. The estates of John of Gaunt, known as the Duchy of Lancaster, which were immense, included a group of Norfolk manors consisting of Gimingham and its neighbouring parishes and Aylsham. Aylsham was the headquarters for these Duchy lands in Norfolk and this must have increased its importance. It was also a centre for the textile industry in the fourteenth and fifteenth centuries and this too helped its growth; the famous 'Aylsham green' cloth was made in the area.

The main road to Norwich seems to have left the market place via Hungate, an important street as the 1624 survey shows. The road then dropped down to the Mermaid beck[1] at Bolwick and then crossed Marsham parish and the then heaths to Norwich. It is odd that the rental does not refer to the Norwich road, only Marsham 'gapp'. In the period when the Bishop of Norwich, John Jegon, who died in 1617/18, lived at the Manor House in Aylsham the Norwich road must have been busy with those on ecclesiastical business between the rest of the Diocese and Aylsham. The county quarter sessions in Norwich must also have led to much use of the road by those on legal business travelling to Norwich as well.

In the 1620s, as now, Aylsham was the centre for a prosperous farming area in which wheat for bread and barley for malt were the main crops. Cattle would be reared and fattened on the meadows and pastures by the river. The spinning of yarn and the weaving of worsted cloth together with all the subsidiary textile crafts, although not as important as in previous centuries, must still have made a significant contribution to the prosperity of the town.

Note

1. Called 'Hendbeck' in the Aylsham rental.

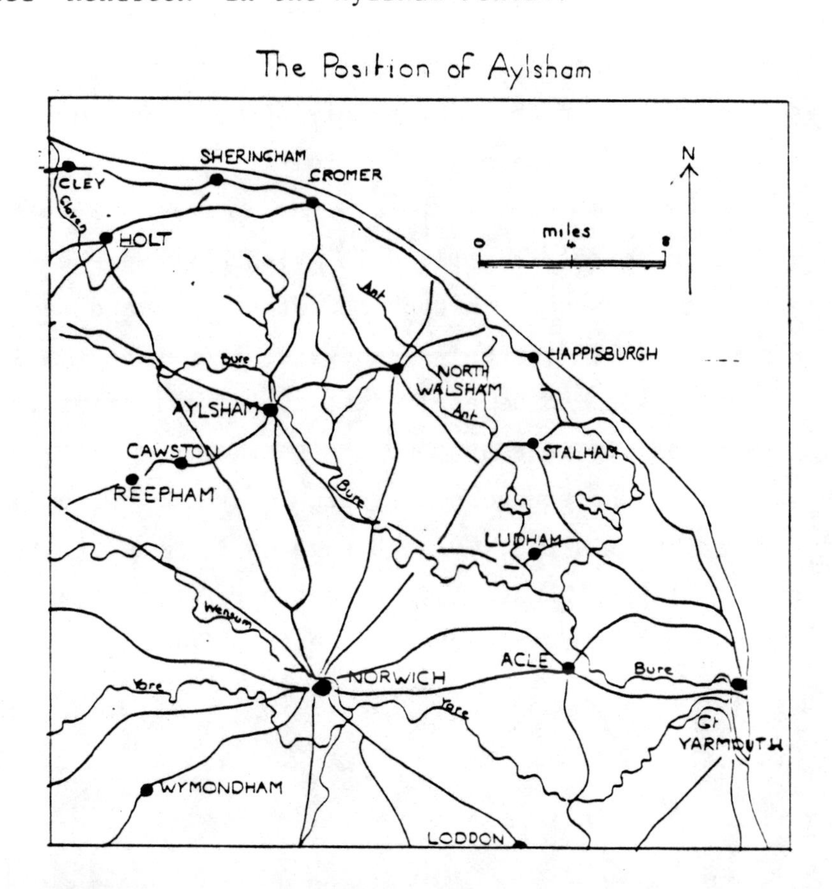

MAP - THE PARISH OF AYLSHAM IN THE SEVENTEENTH CENTURY

Aylsham parish, consisting of 4,102 acres, is a large one. It stretches from Cawston in the west to the River Bure in the east and from the Mermaid, a tributary of the Bure in the south, to Blickling parish in the north. A curious extension of the parish jumps the river Bure in the north-east to include the Abbots Hall area. This was a manor belonging to the abbey of St Edmund in Bury until the dissolution in the 1530s. The valley of the Mermaid and that of the Bure means that meadow land borders the parish to its north, east and south. The western edge is sandy heathland and Abel Heath still survives as open heath. There were larger tracts of heath in the seventeenth century and Stonegate Heath was a large such area in the south-west of the parish.

A network of tracks spread out from the market place into the fertile farmland around it to the east, south and west. The East Field and the West Field were surviving areas of common openfield in the early seventeenth century and the rental has many references to lands in both these fields. On the southern edge of Aylsham parish lay Bolwick, a separate manor and hamlet which had its own area of arable land called Bolwick Field. The records of Aylsham Sextons (Wood's) Manor make it clear that there were bits of surviving medieval common fields in the extension of the parish over the river.

The term 'gate' is applied in Aylsham to several of the roads and streets. It is usually thought to reflect a Scandinavian influence in place names. These 'gates' - Woodgate, Stonegate, Millgate, Hungate, Drabblegate - seem to be applied to sub-divisions of the parish and their exact origin in that context is still not fully understood. Hungate marked the southern approach to the town from Norwich; Millgate was the way out via the 'Great Bridge of Aylsham' to the north although the road to Ingworth must also have been important and seems to have been known as either Netherhall Street or Churchgate.

From the evidence of the rental, Red Lion Street, White Hart Street, Town Lane, Palmers Lane, Buttlands and Schoolhouse Lane did not exist as names in the seventeenth century and this makes a full understanding of this detailed layout of Aylsham in the 1620s quite difficult to unravel.

MAP - THE MANOR OF AYLSHAM LANCASTER AS REVEALED BY THE 1624 RENTAL

The main text of this booklet is a transcription and translation of the rental of the manor of Aylsham Lancaster which was carried out in 1624. The map is an attempt to show the approximate locations of some of the places and buildings mentioned in the survey. The twelve messuages/tenements shown as lining Hungate, for example, are located where buildings that probably survive from that date are now located. The two other Aylsham manors - those of Aylsham Wood (Sexton's) and the Vicarage Manor also had properties in Aylsham town. The Vicarage Manor certainly had some holdings in Hungate. The Vicarage Court Book of 1728 - 80 (NRS 16628 37G) - refers to a cottage in Hungate Street and a tenement in Hungate Street in 1740, on pages 109 and 112 respectively. Hungate clearly had more properties in it than this manorial map might suggest.

The 1624 rental makes no mention of Red Lion Street or White Hart Street either. These names of public houses may date from later. The description of the street leading from the market place of Aylsham to the Great Bridge of Aylsham (Manor of Aylsham Wood Court Book 1623-1660 NRS 16632 37G f 460) could of course include both these roads and certainly White Hart Street if Red Lion Street is treated as having been the east side of the market! The manor of Aylsham Wood clearly had a lot of property in Millgate Street (Court Book 1623-1660, as above, f 459).

This also begs the question of the market place as against the Old Market. The latter has been placed west of the present market place and within the triangle of what are now Schoolhouse Lane, Blickling Road and Church Terrace. The market stalls and market shops have all been placed with reference to the present market place because the old market would seem to have been defunct by 1624. The manor of Aylsham Lancaster was the major manor in Aylsham and the market place lay within its jurisdiction so that all the stalls and shops of the town were within the control of that manor.

Two major areas of Aylsham's agricultural system that are frequently referred to in the survey are the East and West fields. The approximate areas of these have been shown on the parish map.

Whilst the rental of 1624 throws a lot of interesting light on a large part of the parish of Aylsham it is clear that parallel work needs to be carried out on the records of other manors in order to throw more light on the rest of the parish.

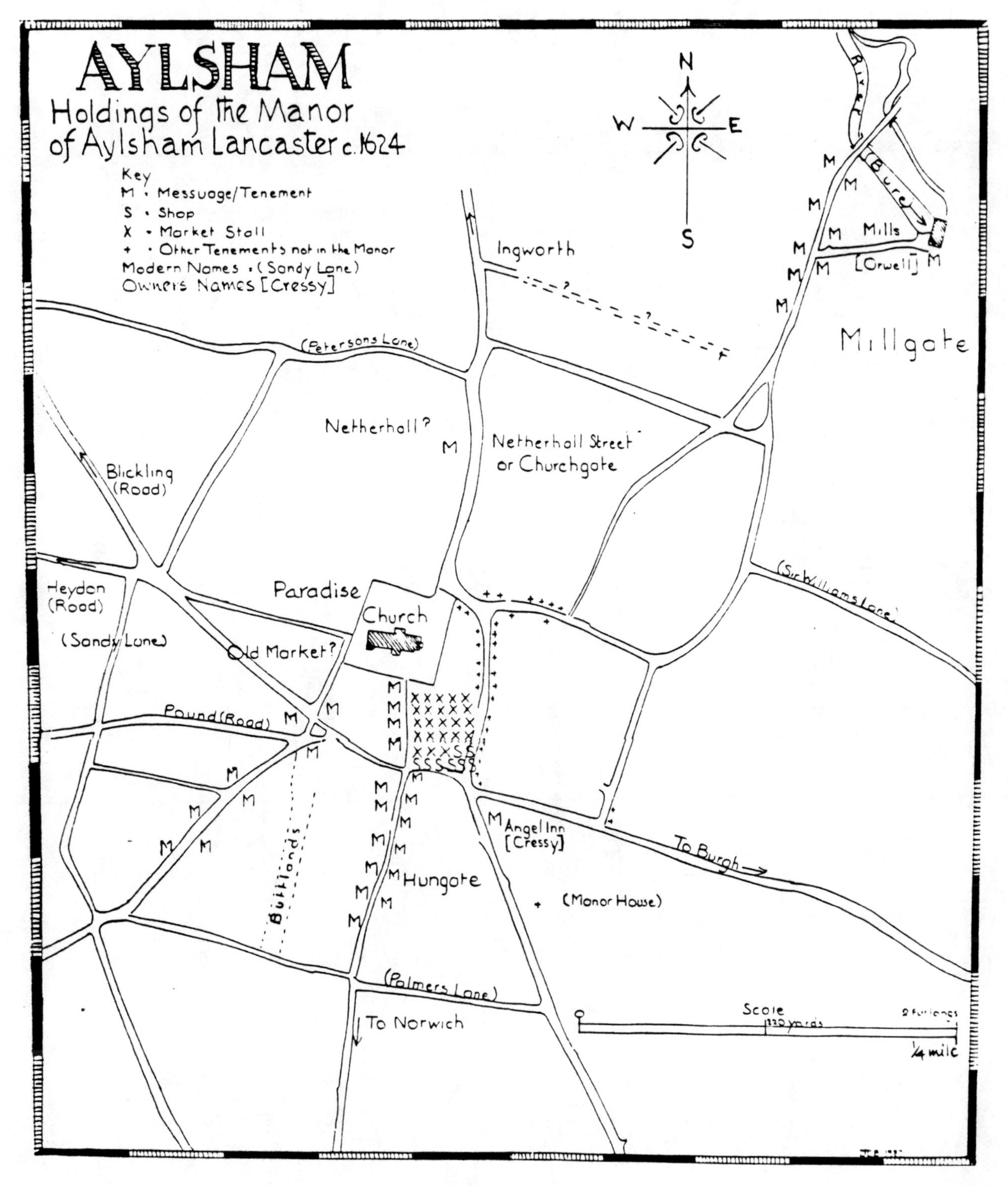